Seriously Bad
album covers!

Seriously Bad album covers!

NICK DIFONZO

NEW HOLLAND

CONTENTS

INTRODUCTION   10
WHERE CAN I FIND FORGOTTEN RECORDS?   13

1 OUR CHILDREN, OUR FUTURE 14
Chinese Racers 15
Ding Dong School 16
Where Did You Come From 17
Circus In Town! 18
Un Dia Con Mamá 19
Kiddie Au Go-Go 20
Amen! 21
Shiver My Timbers! 22
A Place of Our Own 23

2 COUNTRY BOYS 24
Winnin' Country 25
I'm a Nut 26
Bendin' Rules & Breakin'
  Hearts 27
All-Time Country
  Favorites 28
The Wildest Show
  in Texas 29
Julie's Sixteenth
  Birthday 30
My Grass is Green 31
Hoss, He's the Boss 32
Whooooo Boy!!! 33

3 ON THE DANCE FLOOR 34
Cha Cha 35
Everybody Twist 36
Limbo! 37
Let's Hula 38
Dance Into Your Sultan's Heart 39
Saturday Night Fiedler 40
My First Disco Album 41
The Ethel Merman Disco
  Album 42
A Mover "El Esqueleto" 43

4 DON'T ASK, DON'T TELL 44
Caution! Men Swinging 45
 Wet Jam 46
  Rugby Songs Volume Two 47
  An Evening at the Pump Room 48
  Waking and Dreaming 49

Let Me Tell You about My Operation 50
Por Primera Vez 51

5 GETTIN' FUNKY 52
Concerned Party No 1 53
Zip Zap Rap 54
The Negro's Back 55
Fat Boys 56
What The Hell Is This? 57
The Soul of Kijana Unfolds in Music 58
Superstar 59
Crazy Noise 60
The Many Facets of Roger 61

6 GROUP FASHION 62
Waitin' Longin' Yearnin' 63
Country Church 64
God's Only Son 65
Erin's Lovely Home 66
Country Time 67
Naturally 68
I Believe In Music 69
Jesus is a Soul Man 70
Add A Little Beauty To The World 71

7 LOUNGE AXE 72
Live! 73
Présenté par Holiday Inn 74
Elanco Presents The Jack Evans Trio 75
Let's Go Dancing! 76
A Nite Cap With Larry 77
Memories of Elvis 78
A Bold Knight 79
Live 80
The Stellar Unit 81
Rotsa Ruck 82
Rare and Well Done 83

8 DIY 84
How to live with yourself… 85
Think and Grow Rich 86
The Challenge of A Pro 87
How to stop smoking without using willpower 88
Viva Les Crêpes 89
On Course, On The Glide Path 90

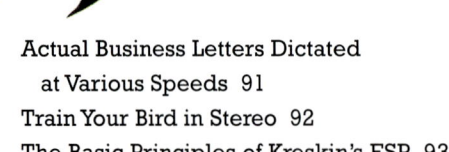

Actual Business Letters Dictated
  at Various Speeds 91
Train Your Bird in Stereo 92
The Basic Principles of Kreskin's ESP 93

9 MUSIC TO... 94

Songs for Bashful Lovers 95
Stereo Dynamics! To Scare Hell
  Out of Your Neigh-bors 96
Music for Washing and Ironing 97
Music to Recline By 98
Music to Grow Plants 99
Music for Bathroom Baritones/
  Bathing Beauties 100
Music to Eat Pizza By 101
Music to Soothe That Tiger 102
Music to Love By 103
Music to Paint By 104
Music for Non Thinkers 105

10 AWFULLY NICE PEOPLE 106

You're Welcome Here 107
Until Sunrise 108
Joyce 109

Now Let Me Sing 110
Look To The Good Side 111
Jacque 112
Come On Down 113
Our Hearts Keep Singing 114
Sing Live Again 115
I've Got Confidence 116
Lost In His Love 117

11 NEVER TOO OLD 118

A Musical Essay on Dixieland Jazz 119
Music Boxes and Chiming
  Clocks 120
Let Me Touch Him 121
Old Fashioned Gospel Singing 122
Knees-Up Party 123
Come To The Chapel 124
Songs That Mom and Dad
  Taught Us 125

12 ORGAN FASCINATION 126

Organ Fascination 127
Organ Moods for Listening 128
Live at the Lamplighter Inn 129

The Mightiest Wurlitzer 130
The Piano Artistry of Jonathan
   Edwards 131
The Majesty of the Big Pipe Organ 132
A Carle-Load of Hits 133
Organ Moods in Hi-Fi 134
Organ Freakout! 135

13 POLKA PARTY 136
For All My Friends 137
Oh Yeah! It's Payday at a
   Polka Party 138
      Lots of Love & Peace 139
         Goin' Bankin' 140
            My Polish Girlfriend 141
            40 20 35 Polka 142
            Now Coal Mines are
            Closing Polka 143

14 ROCKERS 144
   Bricks 145
   Supernature 146
Furr 147
Rollin' Thunder 148

Schizophrenic Circus 149
Keep The Dogs
   Away 150
All Day Thumb Sucker 151

15 SAVED MEN 152
The Whole Church Should
   Get Drunk 153
I Wrestled With God! 154
How To Accomplish the Impossible 155
Lord Lubricate My Bones 156
Something Special 157
I've Had a Touch From The Lord 158
Happy Again 159
Special: Dixie Echoes ('66) 160
Kenny Loves Jesus 161
Hell Without Hell – Is It The Grave? 162
Where Are the Dead? 163

16 BAD GIRLS 164
Rich Man's Woman 165
Music to Remember Her 166
Barbershop Ballads 167
I'm in the mood 168

Music for a Strip
Tease Party 169
Back to the S_ _t! 170
Woman of the World 171
How To Get the Most Out Of
Your Stereo 172
I'll Do Anything For
Money! 173

17 THAT'S JUST SILLY 174
Clef Dwellers 175
I Love My Life 176
They Laughed When I Sat Down 177
In Darkest Africa 178
Songs I Sing on the Jackie Gleason
 Show 179
Out of the Blue 180
Rippling Rhythm in Hi-Fi 181
Apache 182
Snack Attack 183
Don't Smoke Dope, Fry
 Your Hair! 184
Las Aventuras de
 Enrique y Ana 185

18 SOUTH OF THE BORDER 186
A Traveler's Guide to Instant Spanish 187
Casate Jose 188
El Duelo del Mayoral 189
Que Siga la Fiesta 190
Dispuesto a Morir 191
Si, Si, Señor Bandido 192
¡Hay Naranjas! 193
North and South of the Border 194
La Bachata del "Bombillito" 195

19 STRETCHING CREDIBILITY 196
:20 Minute Workout 197
Famous Forty Excercises 198
How to Keep Your Husband Happy 199
Aerobics Country Style 200
Gimnasia en su Hogar Volumen 2 201
Jazz Dancing 202
Carpet Square 203
Texercise 204
Fifteen For Fitness 205

20 TEEN DANCE PARTY 206
Swingin' Night People 207

College Drinking Songs 208
Teen Age Dance Party 209
Frat House Party 210
12 Top Hits 211
Hullabaloo Au-Go-Go!!! 212
12 Hit Parade Tunes 213

21 GOING WILD 214
Is it True What They Say About
 Dixie? 215
Thank You For the Dove 216
Basse-Ackwards 217
Stag Party 218
You Gotta Wash Your Ass 219
The Call of the Wildest 220
Rat On! 221
Run Toward the Roar 222
They Said it Couldn't Be Done! 223

22 AROUND THE WORLD 224
Moscow Nights 225
Játék Az Élet… 226
La Peur 227
Understand Your'e Swede 228
Der Jodel–Peppi vom Schliersee 229
Hot Salsa from Japan 230
Tercet Egzotyczny 231
Les 5 plus grosses bêtises des
 Garçons Bouchers 232
Leberkäs' Hawaii 233

23 A VERY VINYL CHRISTMAS 234
Tijuana Christmas 235
White Christmas 236
Yuletide Disco 237
Merry Christmas 238
All I Want for Christmas is My
 Two Front Teeth 239
Christmas from Hawaii 240
A Singer Christmas for the Family 241
Christmas At Our House 242
Welcome to the World of Ann
 Guest Moore 243

**THE 'WHERE ARE THEY NOW?'
 FILE 244
FURTHER INFORMATION &
 ACKNOWLEDGEMENTS 254**

INTRODUCTION

The album cover is dead. Sure, we still have that flimsy little thing that they put into compact disc cases – a shrunken shadow of its vinyl-protecting predecessor. But even now, as a musical format, CDs are rapidly following vinyl down the trail of obsolescence. Many music fans are now getting their new tunes electronically – no disc, no tape, no hard copy at all unless you choose to make one. So where does that leave the album cover? Will tiny two-inch digital pictures be the only visual accompaniment to the music of the future?

Perhaps the impending disappearance of the album/CD cover is part of what lies behind the growing interest in classic album covers. In recent years, numerous books and websites have sprung up, devoted to this once-neglected arm of popular culture; even major museums have had album cover art exhibitions. Many of the fans of this artwork are members of the 'download generation': not only have they never owned a new vinyl record, but they probably don't even buy CDs any more. It would seem that younger music fans can listen to new music, while still appreciating old album covers from artists they may not even know.

Even if the album cover is gone, never to return, as a collector I'm not worried! The simple fact is

LEFT: Many groups had unique and often frightening fashion sense.

RIGHT: Christmas is a time for family, gift-giving and strange album covers.

that there is no shortage of album covers out there for collectors to discover. Long-Playing 'LP' records were made roughly from 1948 until 1988 – 40 years of music from all genres and all nations, from major releases to home-made curiosities. Millions of different titles, each with their own cover, and most of them are still out there somewhere. Not in a museum or library, but packed in boxes in attics, garages, and basements, waiting for the next spring clean. Old albums are a staple of charity and second-hand stores, and garage sales everywhere. I, for one, don't see them disappearing any time soon.

I consider myself a collector of 'forgotten' records. Not all records are forgotten, of course. In addition to the thousands of classic titles re-issued on CD, tens of thousands more are written about and listed in collectors' value guides. These are the records that generations of collectors have traditionally sought. And then there are the forgotten records. Naturally, most are musical recordings, while others might be speeches, sermons, field recordings, advertisements or just about any other recordable sound. They're rarely re-issued, written about or available for internet download. Many of the artists or producers have faded into obscurity. But the record album remains – a permanent relic of a moment in time, a musician's dream, a salesman's folly or a crackpot's theory.

LEFT: No activity was too mundane to have its very own mood music record.

Most record collectors are looking for good music. Others, like myself, are more interested in the whole package. The sound, the concept and, of course, the cover are all important! This is how collecting bad album covers came about for me. I found that strange, obscure and often tasteless records were a much more interesting thing to collect, even if the contents weren't always worth listening to. Don't get me wrong, I like good music! But most good music is still readily available on CDs or the internet. When it comes to collecting records, I'm looking more for an interesting object in its own right, rather than just the sound recorded on the vinyl. Any collector, whether of coins, dolls or Star Wars figures, can understand that the joy of holding a physical object in your hand can never be replaced by a photograph or digital sound file.

RIGHT: To sell an uncool accordion record, one must 'think outside the box'.

WHERE CAN I FIND FORGOTTEN RECORDS?

One question I am often asked is where to find bad album covers and other strange records. This may vary according to where you live, but I have made up a handy guide to get you started.

Garage/Car Boot Sales:
You never know what might turn up when someone's having a good house clearance. Avoid houses that have sales every year – they got rid of the records long ago.

Charity/Thrift Stores:
These are often a dumping ground for stuff that people just can't throw away. Luckily, few people have the heart to throw away old records. Look out for stores that put records out straight from the donation box without filtering them. You might find someone's entire collection of great – or awful – records.

Second-hand Record Stores:
Yes, they still exist, though they do tend to be expensive. Head to the boxes of 'junk records' – usually shoved underneath the shelves. That's where the forgotten records live.

The Internet:
This is the best place if you're looking for a specific record. However, there's often no picture, the condition can be a mystery, and postage/packaging costs can be ridiculous.

Other Collectors:
Here's a method I don't use as often as I should. Instead of passing up a record you already own, why not buy it and trade it with a fellow collector?

As you can see, there are countless vinyl records still to be found and collected 'in the wild'. And don't worry, you can collect records and listen to MP3s, too…

The album cover is dead! Long live the album cover!

1

Our Children, Our Future

Children occupy a special place in our society. When bad things happen, we're always admonished to 'think about the children'. It would seem that unfortunate events are worse when they happen to kids. A guy has his car stolen? Bad. A kid has his toy car stolen? Worse. Likewise, good things seem to be better when they happen to kids. Grown man with an ice cream cone? So what? Kid with an ice cream cone? Aww.

So our society loves its children. Why, then, do we insist on embarrassing, manipulating and scaring the wits out of them with the records we make for them?

OUR CHILDREN, OUR FUTURE • 15

artist **VARIOUS ARTISTS**
title **Chinese Racers**

I have no idea what this record is supposed to be but it certainly looks like fun! Who sings – the giraffe, the clown or the kids? Unfortunately, the record was missing from the sleeve, so I'll never know. I wonder if they let the kids keep the pedal cars?

16 • OUR CHILDREN, OUR FUTURE

artist **MISS FRANCES**
title **Ding Dong School**

Before there were Special Needs classes, there was Ding Dong School. Miss Frances ran the class with an iron fist and, if you got out of line, she'd slap you sideways with her ding dong bell. When not singing their theme song, the kids enjoyed a rousing chorus of Chuck Berry's 'My Ding-A-Ling'.

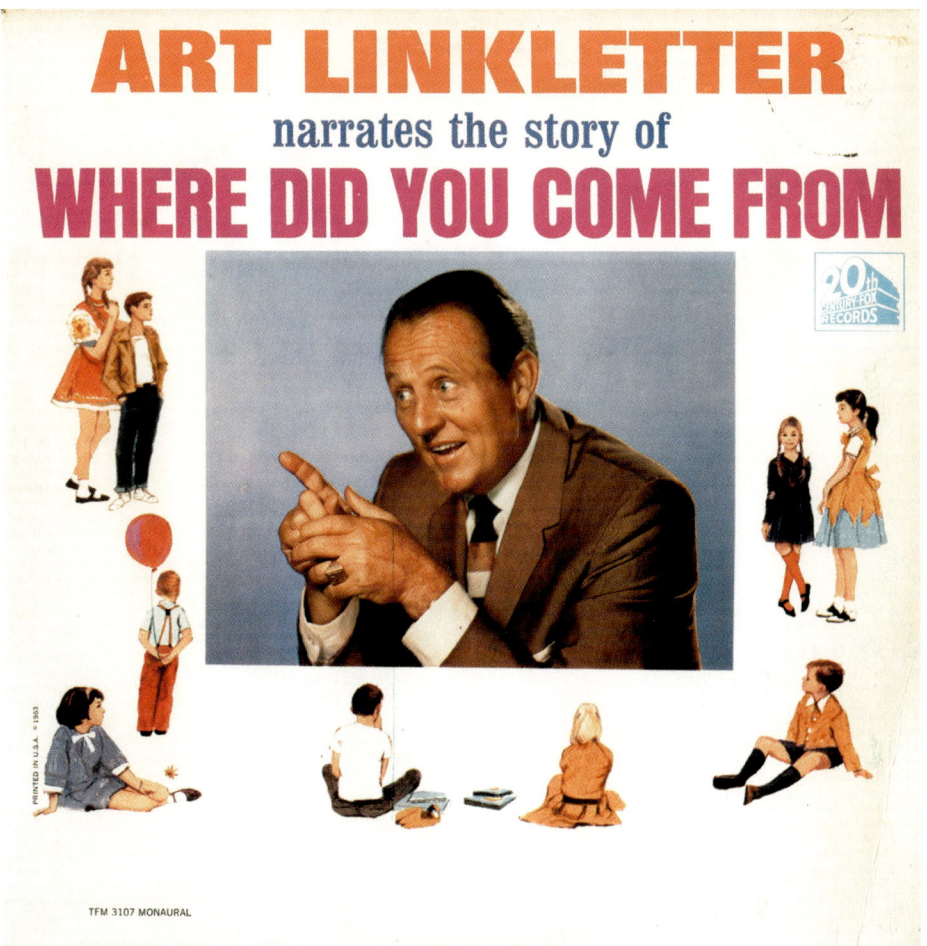

artist **ART LINKLETTER**
title **Where Did You Come From**

They invented automatic bread toasters, automatic dishwashers and automatic tumble dryers. Now here's the automatic sex education class. Yes, no need to bother yourself with those pesky birds and bees – the nice man on television will explain everything!

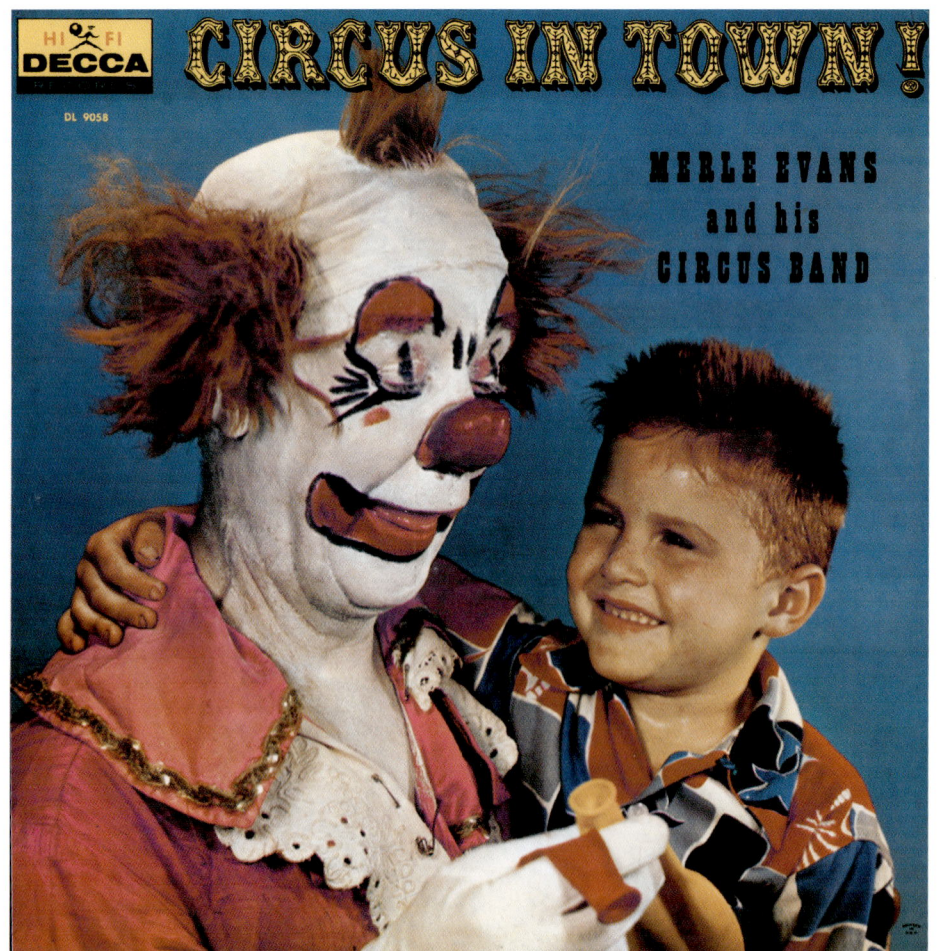

artist **MERLE EVANS AND HIS CIRCUS BAND**
title **Circus In Town!**

Is it really any wonder that every time a clown appears in a modern movie or television programme, he's up to no good? No exaggerated creepiness is needed here. The stubbly face, the droopy makeup, the threadbare outfit – it's all real. I don't think clowns of this era were supposed to be seen close-up.

artist **CEPILLIN**
title **Un Dia Con Mamá**

Here's another clown – different country, different decade, just as scary. Add a Freudian fixation on his mother, and you have an awesomely bad album cover! Cepillin, which means 'little toothbrush', was a dentist before becoming host of a famous children's television show.

20 • OUR CHILDREN, OUR FUTURE

artist **THE MOD MOPPETS**
title **Kiddie Au Go-Go**

Hey, all you hip kids! You're never too young to get on the groovy tip, and this wacky wax is here to help. The moptops will swing till they drop with these super sounds around. Don't be slow, 'cause before you know it, they'll have hair down to their ass and be smoking grass!

artist **ERICK & BEVERLY MASSEGEE**
title **Amen!**

Believe it or not, there is an entire sub-genre of ventriloquist dummy records out there. I guess you just had to imagine the handler's perfect unmoving lips. In any case, this particular one stands out for me because of the sheer ickyness of the picture.

artist **CAPTAIN HOOK AND HIS CHRISTIAN PIRATE CREW**
title **Shiver My Timbers!**

Poor Captain Hook. He was born to be a pirate, but lived in land-locked Indiana. This record originally came with a map to buried treasure hidden in the Bahamas somewhere. It's probably still there! As the good captain says: 'If ye be the matey that discovers it first, write me at the port where I be known as a landlubber!'

artist **MISTER ROGERS**
title **A Place of Our Own**

Who wouldn't want to live in Mr Rogers' street? The houses are neat as pins, the streetcar is always on time and the trees are pruned to perfection. Mr Rogers hovers overhead, making sure that you're properly dressed and change your shoes before coming inside.

2

Country Boys

Country music has always been one of the best-selling genres in America. It's no wonder, then, that country album covers run the gamut from beautiful to unusual to downright bad. From big-time Nashville stars to farm boys still wet behind the ears, bad album covers abound.

Sometimes, country artists are authentic country boys. To them, wearing boots and a cowboy hat is akin to a stockbroker decking himself out in a suit and tie. In other cases, these 'country boys' seem to be more like creations of a big city record company trying to fill a marketing niche. With a crisp western shirt, spit-shined boots, and a gleaming Stetson, these fellas look like they stepped out of a cowboy fashion magazine. 'All hat and no cattle', as the saying goes!

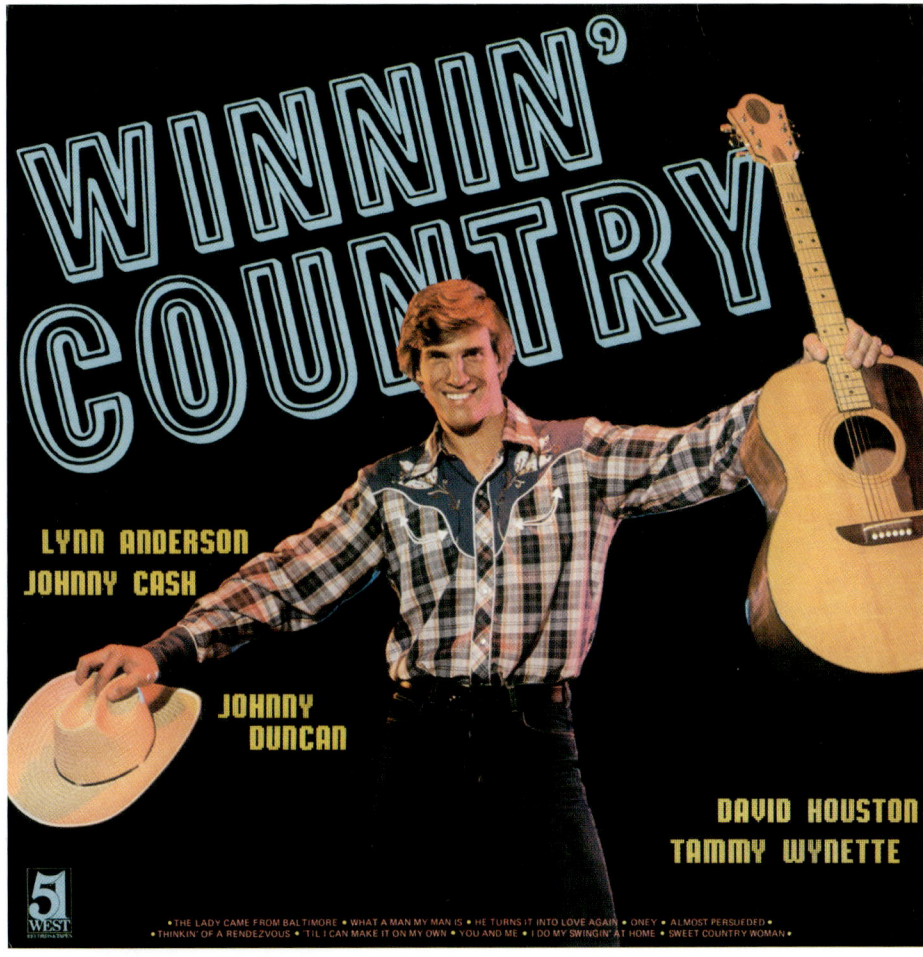

artist **VARIOUS ARTISTS**
title **Winnin' Country**

This guy is about as 'country' as a New York subway car. He agreed to wear the shirt and Wranglers, but there's no way he's messing up his $50 haircut with that nasty hat. This looks like the kind of record you'd buy at a truck stop, if your truck has a turntable, that is!

artist **LEROY PULLINS**
title **I'm a Nut**

Well go-lly! Leroy has the whole 'Gomer Pyle' look down pat. Like the other kids at summer camp, his underwear, shirts, and guitar are clearly labelled. He may be a nut, but he's no fool. Shazam!

artist **HIGH NOON**
title **Bendin' Rules & Breakin' Hearts**

Here we have one of those confused country/rock combos. The leather pants say 'rock 'n' roll' while the bolo ties and fringe jackets say 'country'. To confuse things, the broken chain link fence says 'hip hop'. Fortunately, the classic mullet hair seems to transcend genre.

28 • COUNTRY BOYS

artist **BOB KAMES**
title **All-Time Country Favorites**

Like my Grandpa used to say, you know you've found the right woman when she'll bait your hook with a smile on her face! No, he didn't actually say that, but he did advise me to save money by making all of my clothes out of used tablecloths.

artist **BOWLEY AND WILSON**
title **The Wildest Show in Texas**

Wah-hooo! This is how we party in Texas! Lots of screaming, lots of kicking and a guy passed out in the front row. Even an inflatable robot on stage. But wait, something's wrong here... I've searched the entire picture and can't find one single beer bottle.

artist **JOHN BULT**
title **Julie's Sixteenth Birthday**

It's a caption contest: (1) Julie, I got those test results back. (2) Remember how I said it was over between your sister and me? (3) I got a special present for you, out in the back seat of my Cadillac. (4) I think your Daddy's coming – I'd better go hide in the ladies' room.

artist **ROY DRUSKY**
title **My Grass is Green**

It's clear from this picture who wears the pants in this family. My question is who buys the pants in this family? Is that really proper lawn-mowing attire? Roy! You're supposed to be a country singer, not a go-go dancer.

32 • COUNTRY BOYS

artist **HAROLD MORRISON**
title **Hoss, He's the Boss**
Although a tartan suit may not seem like the most appropriate outfit for the cattle farm, Harold makes it look good. I do hope the photographer got danger money for this assignment, not to mention a new pair of boots.

artist **JUSTIN WILSON**
title **Whoooooo Boy!!!**

The state of Louisiana has its own kind of 'country boy', the Cajun. From the land of crawfish and Tabasco sauce, Justin Wilson was largely responsible for showing off this fun-loving culture to the rest of the world. Play this record and you're just a crab-boil away from the bayou!

3

On the Dance Floor

In the 1950s, 'exotic' dances, such as the Rumba, the Hula, and the Mambo, became popular. Budget record producers realized that if you put instructions to the latest dance steps on the cover, the listener would be too busy trying to imitate the steps to notice that the music was second-rate.

Then, in 1960, Chubby Checker performed 'The Twist' on *The Dick Clark Show*, and a worldwide craze was born that would last a decade and spawn countless crazy theme dances.

Although the novelty dance trend eventually petered out, disco soon reared its ugly head, sending a whole new generation of dancers to the record store to learn the moves.

artist **THE ARTHUR MURRAY ORCHESTRA**
title **Cha Cha**

The Arthur Murrays (that's Mrs. Murray having the seizure) were singularly responsible for teaching middle-class America to dance. Despite the fact that they appear to be the last people you'd want to emulate on the dance floor, their step-by-step instructions had the masses moving.

EVERYBODY TWIST

WARREN COVINGTON and his orchestra

DECCA

THE TWIST ■ PEPPERMINT TWIST ■ LET'S TWIST AGAIN
DEAR LADY TWIST ■ TWIST-HER ■ BIG BAND TWIST
MAMA AND PAPA TWIST ■ FOR TWISTERS ONLY ■

DL 4271

artist **WARREN COVINGTON AND HIS ORCHESTRA**
title **Everybody Twist**

The Twist was quite sexy and shocking when it first appeared. After all, it was the first dance you did alone! More importantly, it was a dance that even the most badly coordinated, two-left-footed wallflower could pull off. As this cover shows, it could even be done in high heels!

artist **THE CARIBBEANAS**
title **Limbo!**

The limbo was the latest in a line of exotic, forbidden dances that corrupted the morals of the nation. This dance seems to be just an excuse to see women in compromising positions. Unfortunately, no studies are available confirming the legacy of lower back pain that practitioners were left with.

artist **MAILE SERENADERS**
title **Let's Hula**

The state of Hawaii has created an entire industry from teaching lanky, poorly coordinated 'haoles' how to dance. Although few non-islanders can pull it off, there is no shortage of tourists who want to try. Here's some advice: forget the instructional record and leave the dancing to the professionals!

Dance Into Your Sultan's Heart

STEREO 2877

Belly Dance with **Özel**

The Newest fun way to exercise...and excite! Includes easy-to-follow, illustrated instruction booklet.

ÖZEL RECORDS

ON THE DANCE FLOOR • 39

artist **ÖZEL**
title **Dance Into Your Sultan's Heart**

An authentic belly dance from a pro like Özel can be a beautiful and sensual experience. Actually, I'm just guessing about that. I would also guess that learning the sultry art of belly dancing from an LP is sure to lead to a bedroom disaster of Biblical proportions!

artist **ARTHUR FIEDLER**
title **Saturday Night Fiedler**

Bandleader Arthur Fiedler never met a musical bandwagon he didn't jump on. Of course, few could stand up against the disco juggernaut of the 1970s. If you didn't submit to the mirrored floors and white suits, you weren't going to sell very many records.

ON THE DANCE FLOOR • 41

artist **THE KID STUFF SINGERS**
title **My First Disco Album**

As shown here, even the youngest kids were not safe from the disco craze. This record prepared kids for a lifetime of disco partying. Fortunately, other products from the era such as *My First Drug Experience* and *My First One Night Stand* were not as successful.

THE ETHEL MERMAN DISCO ALBUM

artist **ETHEL MERMAN**
title **The Ethel Merman Disco Album**
From Grande Dame of Broadway to aging disco diva, Ethel could conquer anything. Like everyone else at the time, an artist had to go disco or go home. The disembodied cowboy hat is perhaps an indication of Ethel's true desire: *The Ethel Merman Country Album.*

ON THE DANCE FLOOR • 43

artist **CHICKEN Y SUS COMANDOS**
title **A Mover "El Esqueleto"**

These out-of-control dancers may have needed some help from the Arthur Murrays! The guy just seems to have noticed that his pants are on fire. It's as if the Comandos dragged this couple off the street and onto the dance floor. Dance you fools! Dance as if Chicken himself compels you!

4

Don't Ask, Don't Tell

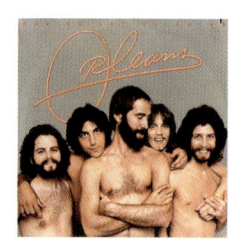

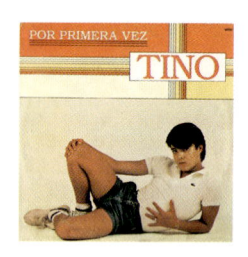

With all the recent controversy concerning gay marriage, gay adoption and homosexuality in general, one might think that gayness appeared on planet Earth sometime in the mid-1970s, around the time of the Village People's first album. Not true! Gay-themed records have actually been around since the earliest days of recorded music. Also, record companies attempted subtle (and not-so-subtle) appeals to gay customers through their cover designs.

Sometimes it can be difficult to tell whether a 1950s' record cover is intentionally appealing to a gay audience or if it's simply our modern sensibilities peeking through!

artist **DENNIS FARNON AND HIS ORCHESTRA**
title **Caution! Men Swinging**

Dennis Farnon's eyes draw us in… Surely he has many stories to tell, most of which you wouldn't want your mother to hear. How many blue collar guys has he swung to the 'other team'? Farnon hovers in front of the construction workers as if to say, 'Another job well done'.

WET JAM

Angel Ferreira

artist **ANGEL FERREIRA**
title **Wet Jam**

When Angel Ferreira invites you out, you're never quite sure where you'll be going. The leather jacket says 'rock 'n' roll', the blinged-out belt buckle says 'hip-hop', and the hair-bow says 'sorority girl party'. I have no idea what the shoulder tassels are saying, however…

DON'T ASK, DON'T TELL • 47

artist **THE JOCK STRAPP ENSEMBLE**
title **Rugby Songs Volume Two**

Rugby players are always going on about their manhood and they certainly show it on this cover. Sure, we all may sing in the shower on occasion, but usually we're alone! So if you hear 'Balls To Your Partner' coming from the men's changing room, you'd better hold it till you get home.

48 • DON'T ASK, DON'T TELL

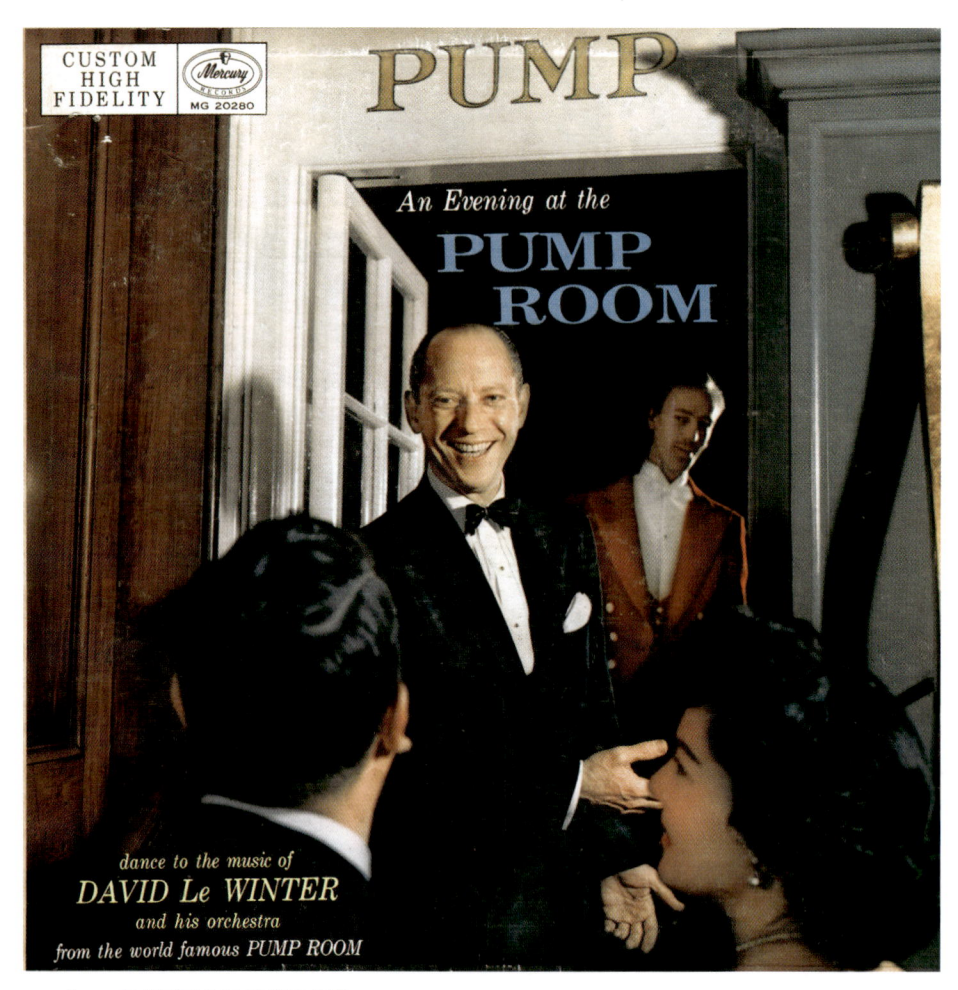

artist **DAVID LE WINTER**
title **An Evening at the Pump Room**

The Pump Room is a legendary Chicago eatery popular with myriad stars of music and film. This cover, however, makes the joint look like a shady basement speakeasy, and the boy in red looks a bit too eager. What exactly do they serve in here, anyway?

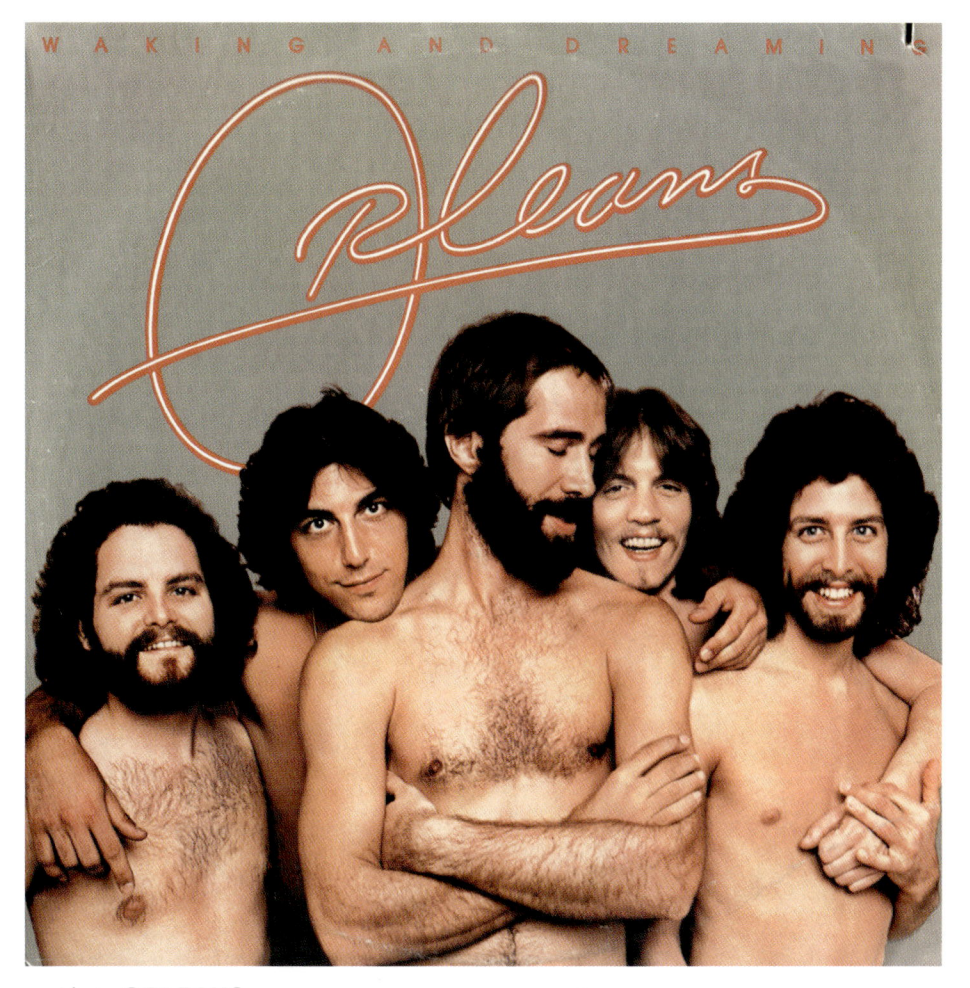

artist **ORLEANS**
title **Waking and Dreaming**

In the 1970s, it appears that the few groups who didn't join the disco trend chose instead to get naked on their album covers. 'If we can't wear polyester shirts, we'll wear nothing at all,' would seem to be the idea. Perhaps they thought their hair would grow long enough to cover their naughty bits?

LET ME TELL YOU ABOUT MY OPERATION

RAE BOURBON SPEAKING . . . . .

UTC 7

HIGH INFIDELITY
A BROAD RANGE RECORDING

artist **RAE BOURBON**
title **Let Me Tell You About My Operation**

This is not the opening line you want to hear when trying to pick up a lady at a club. But it seems cross-dressing crooner Rae (aka Ray) Bourbon plans to tell you all about it. Fine, Rae, if you really have to … but could you keep the towel on?

POR PRIMERA VEZ

TINO

artist **TINO**
title **Por Primera Vez**

Boy-band star Tino certainly knows how to appeal to his fans – and that goes for both the teenage girls and the middle-aged men. Although he looks sweet and innocent, somehow I don't think that posing for a sexy album cover is his 'primera vez'!

5

Gettin' Funky

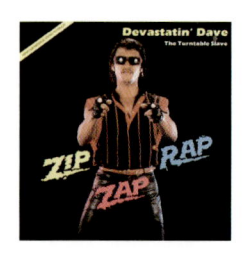

According to the American Heritage dictionary, the first recorded use of the word 'funky' was in 1784 – a word that referred to the smell of old cheese.

Around the turn of the 20th century, the word had taken on sexual overtones, and was considered at best an impolite slang word. In the 1900s, a black bandleader from New Orleans named Buddy Bolden used a song called 'Funky Butt' for his band's theme.

By the 1950s, jazz groups had officially absorbed the word into the culture of black music. They used it to refer to the earthy, rough, and sweaty style that shone through in their music. The Funk was born!

artist **CAPTAIN SKY**
title **Concerned Party No 1**

Meet Captain Sky, the new superhero of funk. With an outfit from Barbarella's garage sale and a cover designed by a 10-year old, this would have to be one awesome record to live up to its cover – and it is!

Devastatin' Dave
The Turntable Slave

HEAR OUR MESSAGE, SAY NO TO DRUGS!

ZIP ZAP RAP

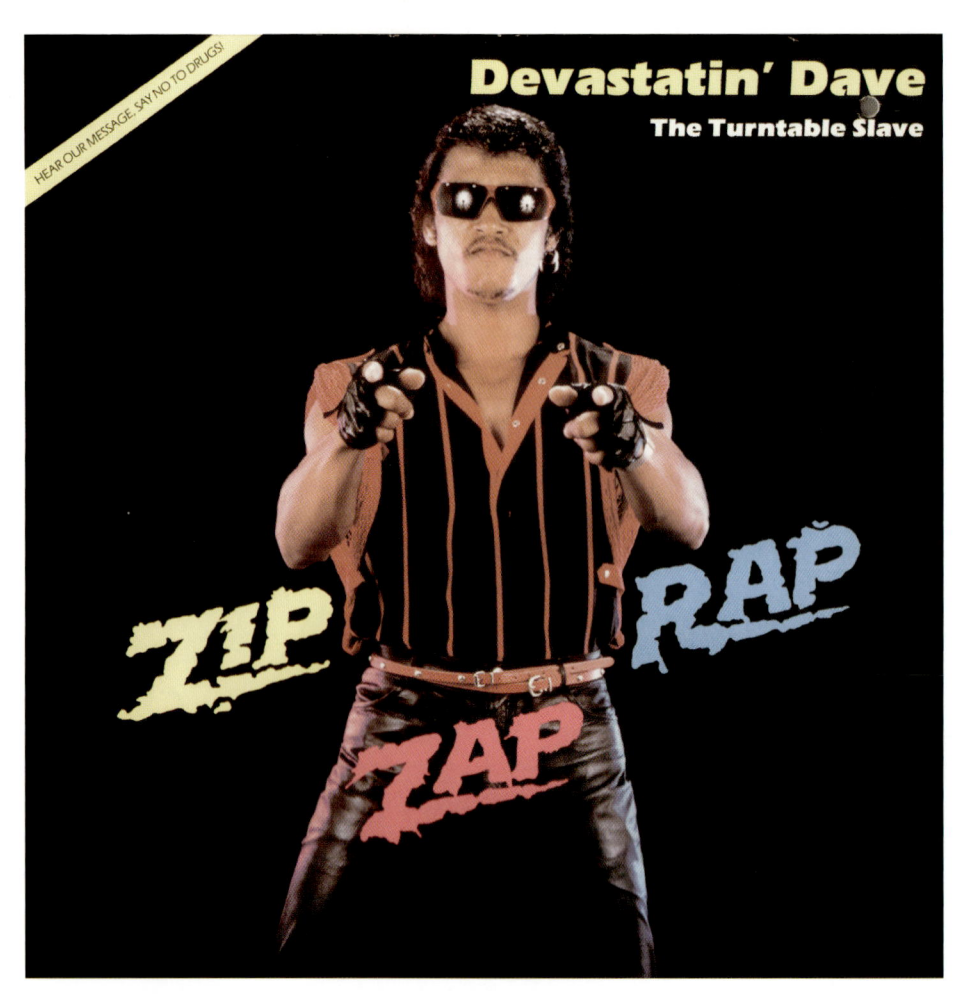

54 • GETTIN' FUNKY

artist **DEVASTATIN' DAVE THE TURNTABLE SLAVE**
title **Zip Zap Rap**
This cover has become quite popular on the internet, and it's easy to see why. Perhaps its Dave's combination of clothing styles that we had all thankfully forgotten about. Don't do drugs, or Dave will open a can of Zip Zap on your ass!

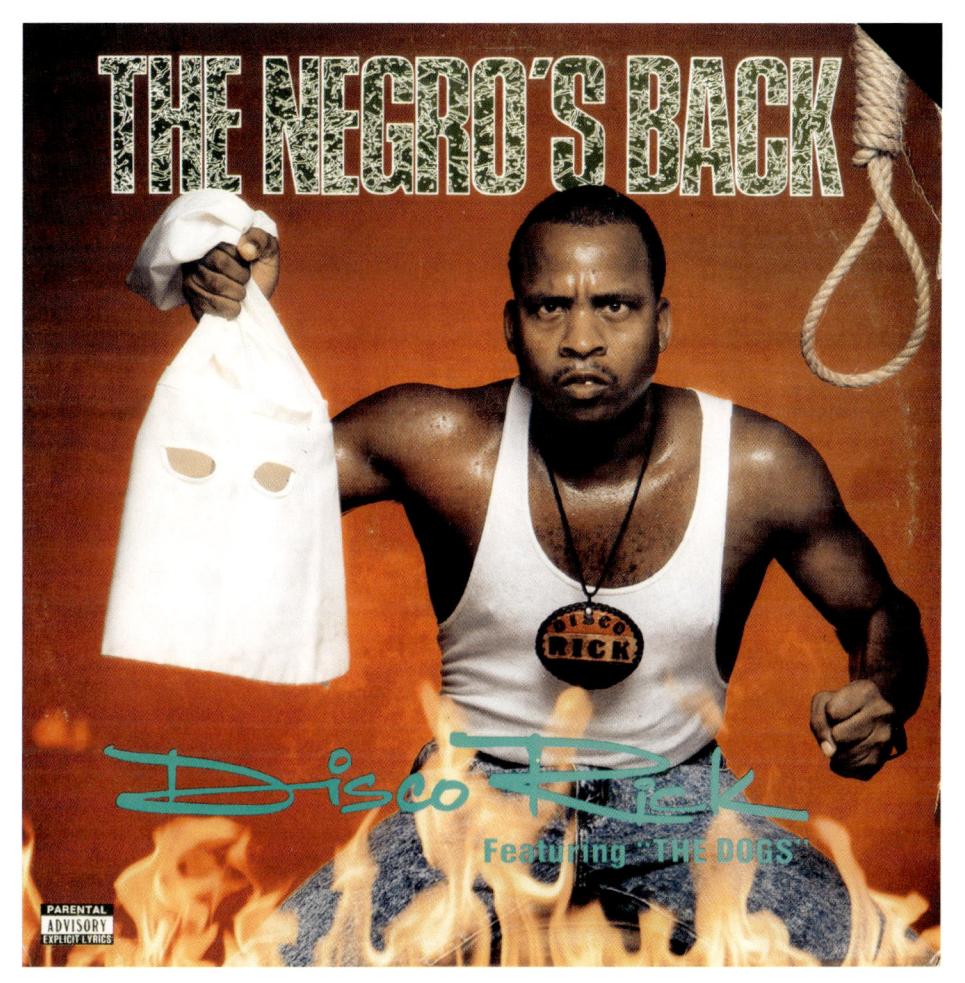

artist **DISCO RICK FEATURING "THE DOGS"**
title **The Negro's Back**
Note to self: Do not anger Disco Rick. Say only nice, happy things about Disco Rick. Talk about what a generous, compassionate man Disco Rick is. Remember, Disco Rick might know where you live!

artist **FAT BOYS**
title **Fat Boys**

You know what's funny? By today's standards, the Fat Boys really aren't all that fat! If they were still around, they'd be called the Big Boned Boys, or perhaps the Overactive Pituitary Boys. Doesn't quite have the same ring to it, does it?

artist **JOHNNY GUITAR WATSON**
title **What The Hell Is This?**

People had different ways of dealing with the gas shortages of the 1970s. Some waited for hours in line for fuel, and others bought more efficient vehicles. Bluesman Johnny 'Guitar' Watson's idea has him pimped out on a tricycle, pushed by a trio of beauties. Not bad!

artist **KIJANA**
title **The Soul of Kijana unfolds in Music**
Soulful crooner Kijana apparently had trouble finding a record company for his album, so he just made it himself. The lettering, the exploding heart logo, the giant bow tie – it's all Kijana. The sharp hairdo is Kijana, too – when not singing, he ran a Los Angeles hair shop.

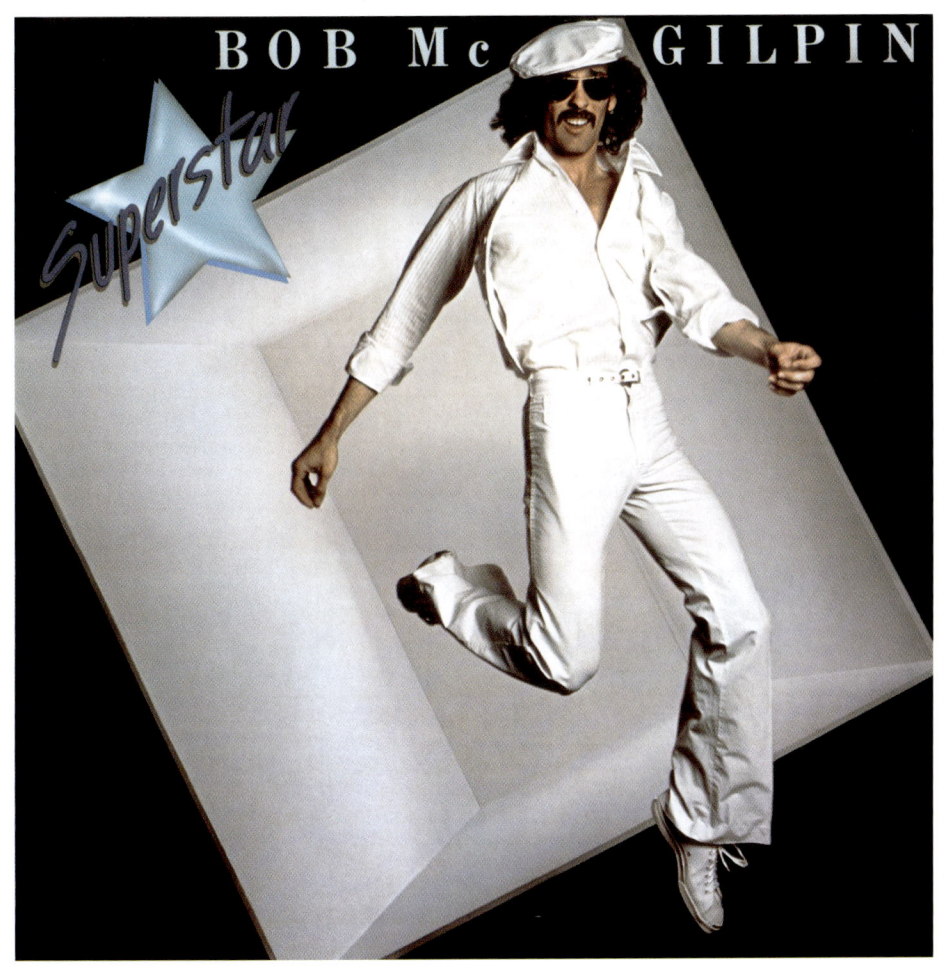

artist **BOB McGILPIN**
title **Superstar**

This guy looks like he's running a marathon on tiptoe. Or maybe he's escaping from a mob of fans – he is a 'superstar' after all… Perhaps I'm just jealous that a man can no longer go out in public in white bellbottoms and a beret without being called 'light in the loafers'.

artist **STEZO**
title **Crazy Noise**

Sometimes it takes an album cover to remind you of bad fashions from the past. In this case, Stezo showcases the 'baggy acid-washed denim with crap written all over it' look that I vaguely recall from my youth. I think the fashion came to an end when people realized you couldn't wash your clothes any more.

artist **ROGER TROUTMAN**
title **The Many Facets of Roger**

He's wacky! He's sexy! He's got his glitter pirate suit and he's ready to go! He's Roger Troutman, disco funkmeister extraordinaire. Roger may have many facets, but why do they all seem to involve shiny suits, polyester, and patchy chest hair?

6

Group Fashion

The first priority of a music group: the instruments. Are the guitars tuned? Is the trumpet shined up? Will the drums fit in the van? The second priority: outfits. Even the largest old-time orchestra wore matching tuxedos, while a doo-wop band might blow the budget to get that perfect look. The Beatles defined the early rock 'n' roll look with sharp suits and skinny ties.

In this chapter, I have mostly chosen covers of Christian groups – not because they are the only ones to indulge in bizarre album cover fashion but simply because records of this genre have been neglected for so long! Not to mention the fact that these groups seemed to have had spectacularly strange taste in fashion…

artist **THE SINGING LEDBETTERS**
title **Waitin' Longin' Yearnin'**

It's never too early to introduce a new member into the family singing group. Here, little Randy had his mini-me suit shined up and ready for the stage. If he proves too short to reach the microphone, he can always use his sisters' voluminous hair to prop him up.

64 • GROUP FASHION

artist **COUNTRY CHURCH**
title **Country Church**
These friendly folks show that you can dress warmly and still be fashionable. Some non-PC people call sleeveless white shirts 'wife-beaters'... Farmers, on the other hand, are known to wear these comfortable 'wheat-beaters'.

GROUP FASHION • 65

artist **THE ROYAL HEIRS**
title **God's Only Son**

Some people need a visit from the fashion police. The Royal Heirs are going to need the whole police department. Potential charges include failure to maintain solid shade, blatant disregard for complementary hues, and gross misuse of a bow tie.

66 • GROUP FASHION

artist NOEL HENRY AND THE CELTIC BLUES
title Erin's Lovely Home

These fellows say they're from Ireland, but they're not fitting the conventional stereotype very well. They're not wearing green, they're not wielding shillelaghs, and they certainly don't have their lucky charms.

GROUP FASHION • 67

The STEFFIN Sisters

Country Time

artist **THE STEFFIN SISTERS**
title **Country Time**

Take two cans of mega-hold hairspray, a bottle of acid-wash and one cup of rhinestones, wrap in gold lamé, sprinkle liberally with fringe and blow dry. Add a lifetime of sororal love and what do you end up with? The Steffin Sisters!

68 • GROUP FASHION

NATURALLY

Sunshade 'n Rain

artist **SUNSHADE 'N RAIN**
title **Naturally**

Sunshade 'n Rain shows our latest line of outdoor gear. Our new 'Drylon' jackets repel moisture as well as attract the ladies, while the 'action ruffles' on our shirts scare away insect pests. Our shoes are specially made to blend in with the snow, and are available in white, grey and yellow.

artist **FOGGY RIVER BOYS**
title **I Believe In Music**
Their choice of fabric reminds me of one of those 3D illusion puzzles where you cross your eyes and see a picture. If you squint and look at the Foggy River Boys, you see… a puppy? A skyscraper? Who knows? I hate those puzzles.

70 • GROUP FASHION

JESUS IS A SOUL MAN
the SEGO BROTHERS & NAOMI

artist **THE SEGO BROTHERS & NAOMI**
title **Jesus is a Soul Man**

Jesus may in fact be a soul man, but how on Earth would these guys know? They look to have about as much 'soul' as a Republican Party fundraiser. But it would seem that no group is above using a witty double entendre to sell a few records!

Add A Little Beauty To The World

The Rhodes Kids

"AMERICA'S NO.1 MUSICAL FAMILY"

GROUP FASHION • 71

artist **THE RHODES KIDS**
title **Add A Little Beauty To The World**
In the battle for top spot in the 'musical family' game, the Rhodes Kids took no prisoners. With outfits imported directly from Polyesterstan, the family clawed their way to the top, on the backs of such Hollywood creations as the Brady Bunch and the Partridge Family.

7

Lounge Axe

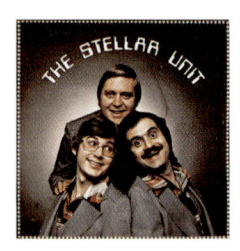

Few bands have received so little credit for their work as the hard-working cocktail lounge acts of the 1970s. Think Murph and the Magictones from *The Blues Brothers*: smarmy disco-electric cover versions of popular hits and old standards on a shag-covered stage.

From the Holiday Inns of Ohio to the Hiltons of Hawaii, hundreds of talented musicians honed their chops playing to vacationing couples and disinterested singles looking for a quick rendezvous. The music was usually a backdrop for a charismatic lead man, who needed to be able to work the crowd, keeping the tables full and the drinks flowing. Often, the only thing we have left to remember these bands by is a souvenir record album.

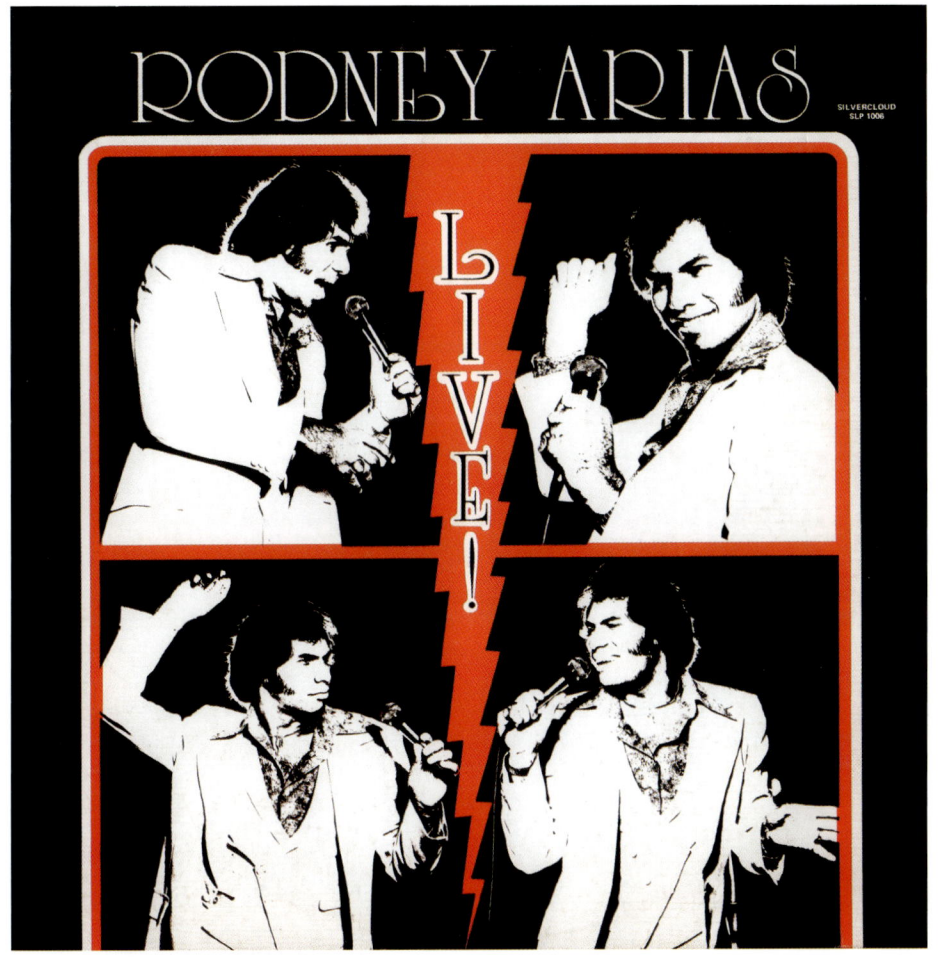

artist **RODNEY ARIAS**
title **Live!**

Rodney obviously had a good time on stage and I'll bet he made sure the audience did too. Though his hair seems to sprout from every available suit opening, his mischievous smile would melt a lady's heart quicker than a Pina Colada in the Hawaiian sun.

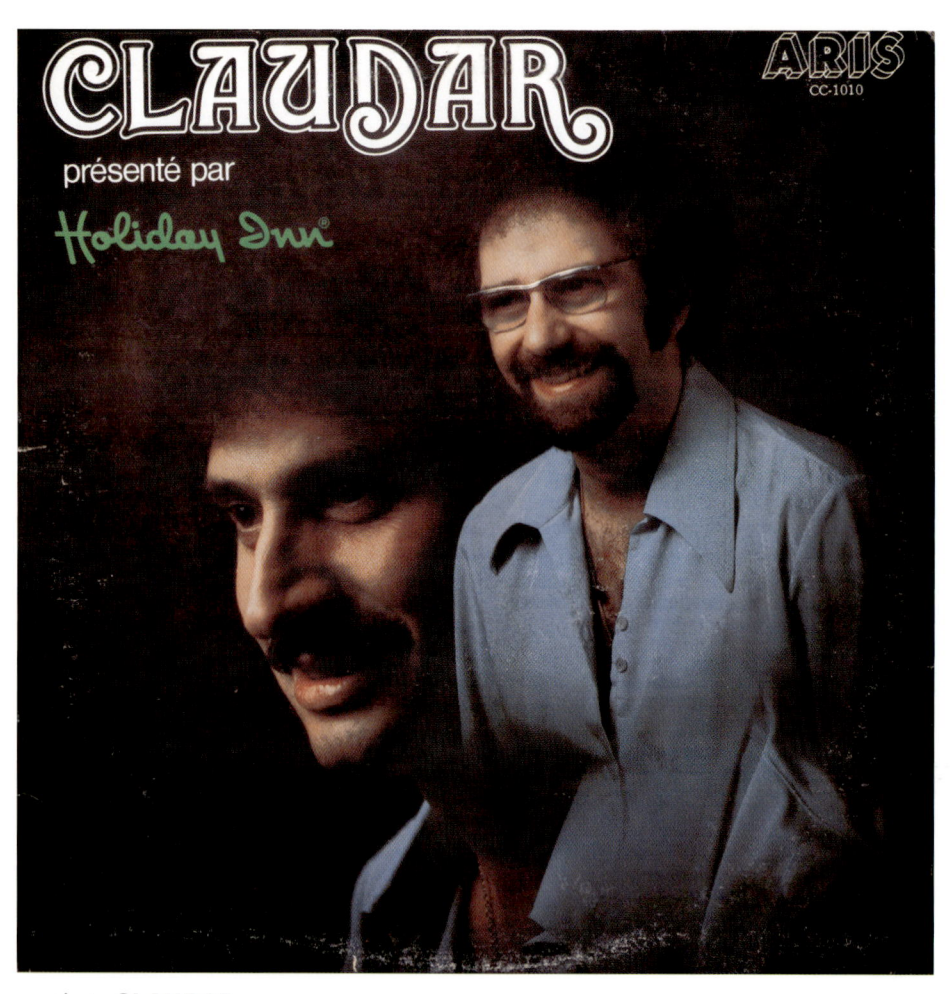

artist **CLAUDAR**
title **Présenté par Holiday Inn**

CLAUDe and ARmando, a lounge duo from Canada, play all the usual suspects: 'Quando Quando', 'Volare', and 'Arrivederci Roma'. One can only imagine the exciting evening of dining, dancing, and hanky-panky that was surely had by the original owners of this disc!

artist **THE JACK EVANS TRIO**
title **Elanco Presents The Jack Evans Trio**

As far as I can tell, this band was put together purely to play at Elanco pharmaceutical company parties. Patti's drum kit is not covered with punk rock stickers, but with company slogans such as 'We Work For Peanuts… And We Are Proud Of It!'.

76 • LOUNGE AXE

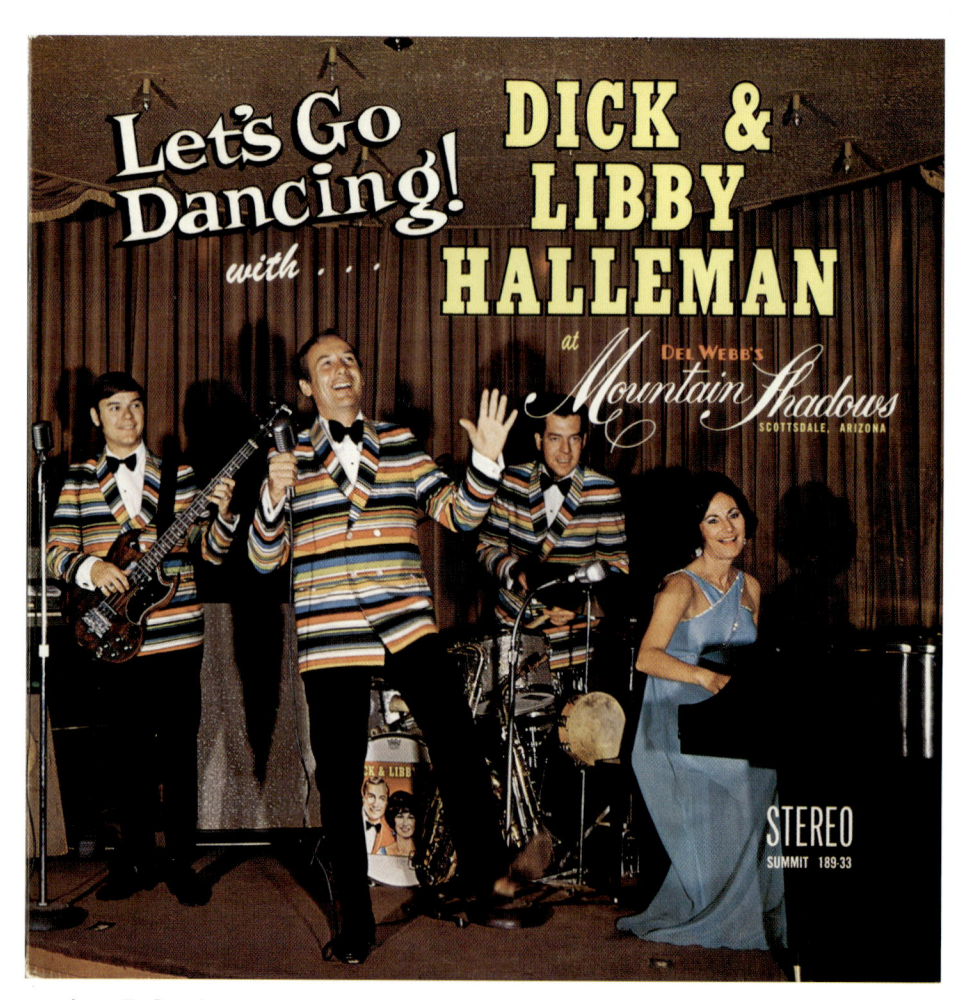

artist **DICK & LIBBY HALLEMAN**
title **Let's Go Dancing!**

The Hallemans really tore it up at Mountain Shadows resort. I can imagine the elderly snowbirds in the audience, trying to escape the winter blues in the Arizona desert. I wouldn't be surprised if they kept an oxygen machine behind the piano for when things got a bit too exciting.

artist **LARRY RIVERA**
title **A Nite Cap With Larry**

It's the perfect evening at the Coco Palms in Hawaii. The drinks are iced and umbrella-ed, the rose petals are properly spread and Larry Rivera is at the mic. After an exhausting day of surfing, shopping and tanning, Larry is just the thing to help you relax.

artist **BOBBIE MILLS FEATURING THE SHADES OF GOLD**
title **Memories of Elvis**

Is he a country singer? An Elvis impersonator? A truck driver? All of the above and more! On the back cover, Bobbie tells us his life story, ALL IN CAPITALS, complete with misspellings. His wife's name is blacked out with pen for some reason. Let's just say this guy is 'all shook up'.

artist **DAVEY BOLD**
title **A Bold Knight**

The full-featured lounge act is truly a lost art form. There was comedy, song and no shortage of scantily-clad women. One imagines that the headliner required a good opening act to get the crowd in the mood and in the drink. Good times, folks, good times.

80 • LOUNGE AXE

BRAVE LP   **STEREO**   **3006**

Sam Venti + Bobby Randazzo =

the PLAYBOY PAIR

"LIVE"

artist   **THE PLAYBOY PAIR**
title   **Live**

The Playboy Pair was a rocking lounge duo from the Chicago area. This record was made at a club called The Foaming 60s, which sounds like a great place to have heard the boys belt out their jazzy covers of the latest tunes.

artist **THE STELLAR UNIT**
title **The Stellar Unit**

In the annals of nerdy record covers, this one takes the 20-sided dice. The polyester print shirts, square glasses, even the retro-futuristic computer font. I don't know much about these guys, but I'd bet that at least one of them could fix my computer.

82 • LOUNGE AXE

artist **ARNIE AND CHISE**
title **Rotsa Ruck**

Here we have a champion cover from the annals of bad taste. After a decade of demonizing the culture of the Japanese during World War 2, this lounge act must have been quite exotic. By today's standards, however, the title is a quite a bomb.

artist **SHARLENE SHARP**
title **Rare and Well Done**

They say 'everything's bigger in Texas,' and that was certainly true at Sonny Look's Sir Loin club. Sonny introduced his ladies in style, and spared no expense. My question is this: is drunk horse-riding legal?

8

DIY

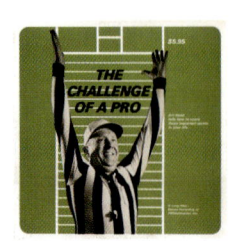

The emergence of long-playing albums was great for bands, but it also meant that records were not just for music any more. Anyone with a crackpot theory and a few thousand dollars could cut a disc.

For those who considered a self-help book to be too much reading, a recorded alternative was just the thing. Many of these would help you get rich or become a successful businessman. Others offered advice on everything from pet training, hypnosis, cooking, golfing, and even choosing the right wine. Although similar products can still be found today, I doubt if we'll see such great covers again!

artist **DR MURRAY BANKS**
title **how to live with yourself...**
Instead of spending your hard-earned money for a trained head-shrinker, try this record instead. Look at all the crazy people in the waiting room! Not like you. You're not crazy, you just need someone to talk to. A kind ear to listen to your troubles. Like this record.

"ANYTHING THE MIND CAN CONCEIVE AND BELIEVE, IT CAN ACHIEVE"

THINK and GROW RICH

SUCCESS MOTIVATION INSTITUTE, INC.
HIGH FIDELITY

THE ESSENCE OF THE IMMORTAL BOOK BY
NAPOLEON HILL
NARRATED BY
EARL NIGHTINGALE

OVER 3,000,000 COPIES SOLD!

artist **EARL NIGHTINGALE**
title **Think and Grow Rich**

Wow, what a concept! Okay, let's give it a try. I think I'll cut my employees' wages in half! Even better… sack the lot of them, and outsource the work to China! Now, I think I'll use poor quality materials and shoddy construction. Now I'm rich! This record works great!

THE CHALLENGE OF A PRO

$5.95

Art Holst tells how to score those important points in your life.

A Long Play— Stereo Recording of PROmotivation, Inc.

artist **ART HOLST**
title **The Challenge of a Pro**
Most retired American football referees spend their days reminiscing about the old days – the great plays, the missed calls. Not Mr Holst! He embarked on the public speaking circuit, telling businessmen how to score touchdowns in the game of life.

RCA LSP-4311　　　　　　　　　　　　**VICTOR** STEREO

How to stop smoking without using willpower

artist **HOWARD LOY**
title **How to stop smoking without using willpower**

I am amazed that this method of smoking cessation never caught on. What could be more appealing to the modern addict? Similarly unpopular was Mr Loy's second record, *How to Stop Stuffing Cheeseburgers in Your Mouth Without Using Willpower.*

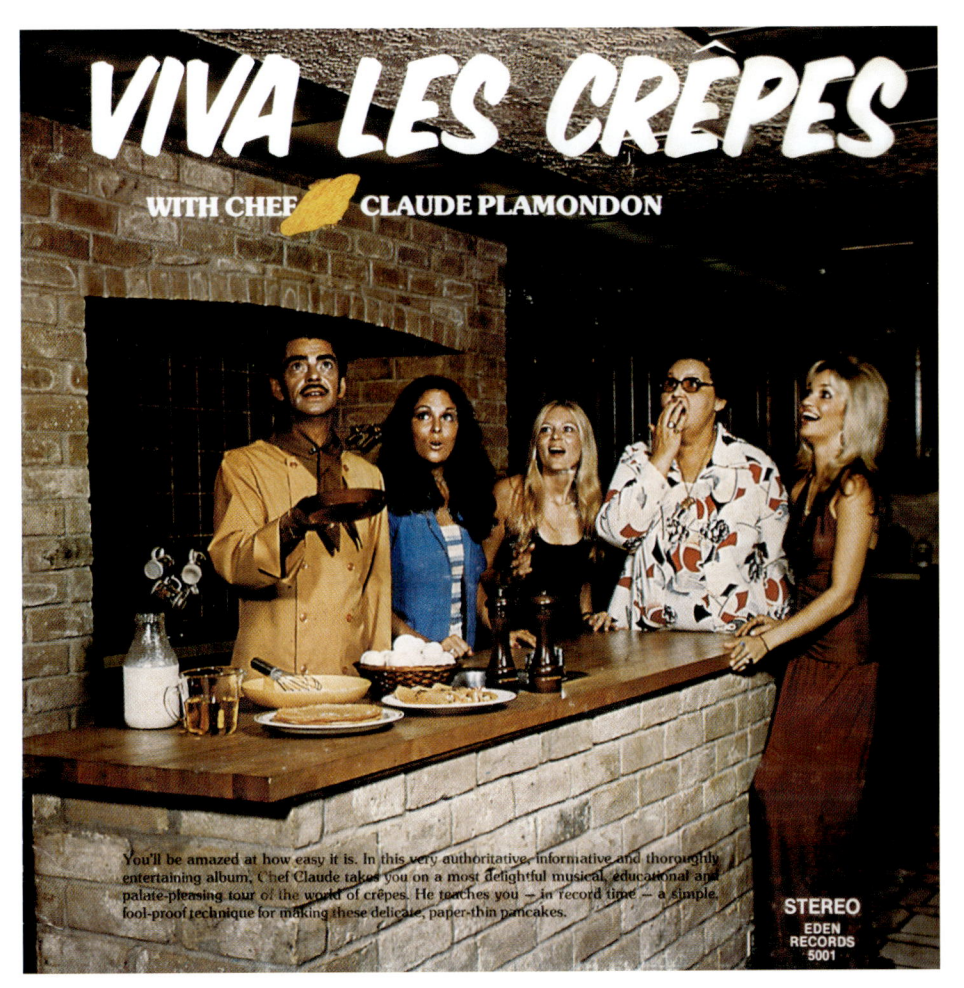

artist **CHEF CLAUDE PLAMONDON**
title **Viva Les Crêpes**

In the days before the planet was inundated with celebrity chefs, Chef Claude was the world's biggest exponent of the crêpe. One flip of his special crêpe-flipping pan could send nearby women into spates of ecstasy. Such is the life of a crêpe chef.

ON COURSE, ON THE GLIDE PATH...

CESSNA 210
COURTESY CESSNA AIRCRAFT CO.

AERO PROGRESS, INC. #7001

artist **AERO PROGRESS**
title **On Course, On The Glide Path**

Learning to fly an aeroplane via record album just doesn't seem safe. Was the student supposed to bring a portable turntable on board, and listen as he flew? I can only imagine what would happen if you got up there only to realize you didn't bring the *How to Land* disc!

artist **STENODISC**

title **Actual Business Letters Dictated at Various Speeds**

This record cover subtlety prepares the student for the hellish life of office drudgery that awaits her upon completion of the course. Plucking out asinine memos on the typewriter. Answering six lines of angry customer phone calls. All the while dreaming of her Elvis records.

artist   **HENRY J. BATES AND ROBERT L. BUSENBARK**
title   **Train Your Bird in Stereo**

There are lots of bird training records out there, all with one problem. They don't train your bird to do anything useful. Now, if you can train my bird to get me a beer from the fridge, or answer the phone when sales people call, then we'll talk. Until then, Polly can keep her crackers to herself.

artist **KRESKIN**
title **The Basic Principles of Kreskin's ESP**

You will buy this record… You will take it home and play it… You will then take all your money and mail it to Kreskin… You are now feeling very sleepy… When you wake up, you will not realize that hypnotism has nothing to do with ESP…

9

Music To...

The 'mood music' craze of the 1950s started innocently enough, with George Melachrino's *Music For Dining*. Not a bad idea. One needs to justify one's purchase of a new hi-fi set, and making the wife happy at dinner is a good start. The record was a huge success, and soon there were records available for every conceivable mood and situation.

Some were useful: *Music to Bathe By*, *Music to Party By*, *Music to Relax By*. Others were silly: *Music For Nervous People*, *Music for Squares*. And some were incomprehensible: *Music to Drill Oil Wells By*, *Music for Cooking With Gas*. Following are some great examples of *Music to Listen to Music By*.

artist **CARL EUGSTER WITH ORCHESTRA**
title **Songs for Bashful Lovers**

It seems to me that if you manage to get the girl back to your house to play this album, you've already won half the battle. What do you need this record for? Put on some Barry White and let the master do his work!

artist **VARIOUS ARTISTS**
title **Stereo Dynamics! To Scare Hell Out of Your Neigh-bors**
If the gibbeted skeletons in your yard weren't enough to make your 'neigh-bors' fit extra locks and additional security features to their doors, then this record promises to do the trick. And I thought that the yapping dog in the back yard was bad…

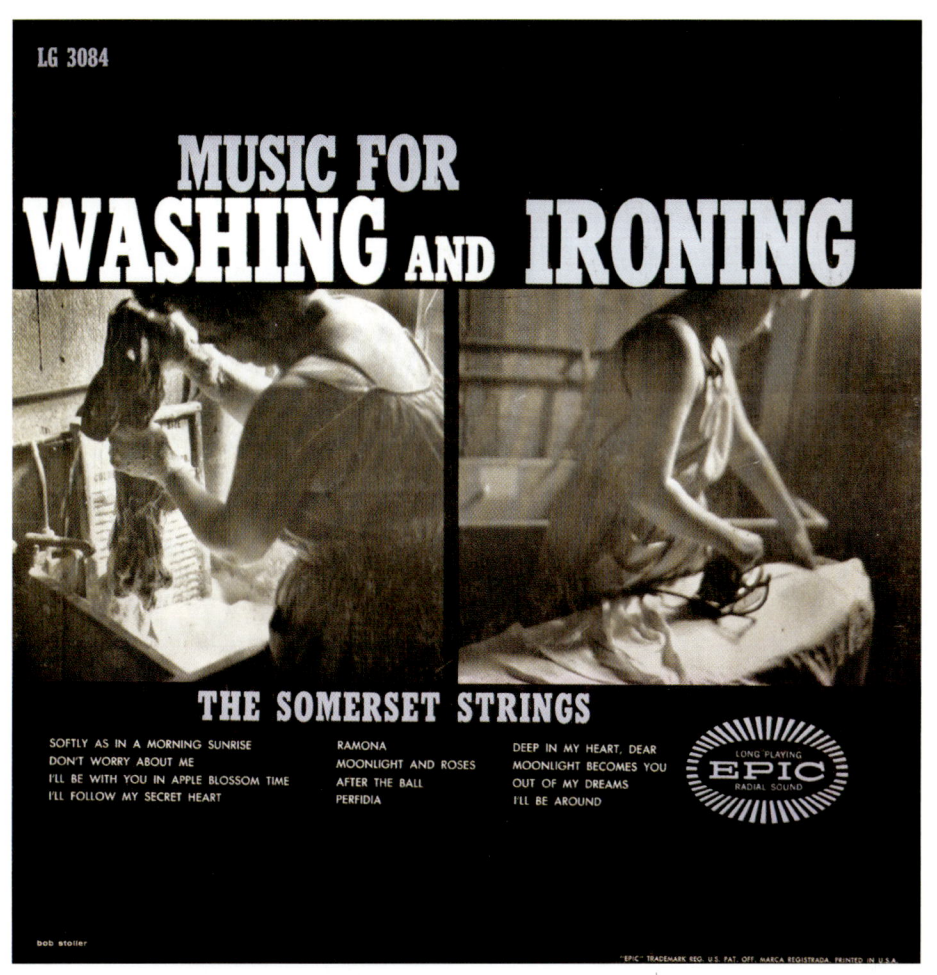

artist **THE SOMERSET STRINGS**
title **Music for Washing and Ironing**

Finally, something for the ladies. Sure, the wife has been bugging you to buy her a washing machine. But why spend the money when you can give her this record instead? She's likely to be so thankful that she may break out *Music for a Strip Tease Party* (see page 169)!

artist **RICHARD MALTBY AND HIS ORCHESTRA**
title **Music to Recline By**

Some things just go great together, like nice music and shiny, fake leather recliners. These chair makers have the right idea. Of course, recliner technology would not be fully realized for several years, until the introduction of cupholders and the in-chair icebox.

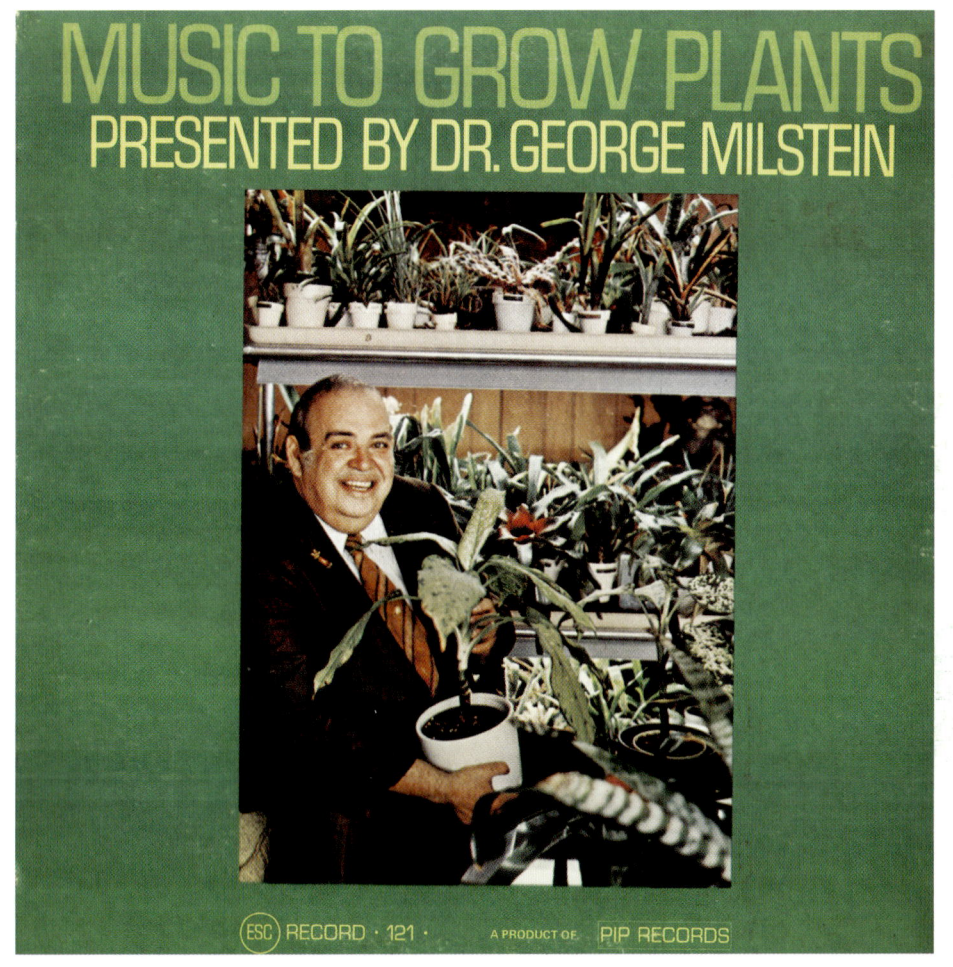

MUSIC TO GROW PLANTS
PRESENTED BY DR. GEORGE MILSTEIN

ESC RECORD · 121 · A PRODUCT OF PIP RECORDS

artist **DR GEORGE MILSTEIN**
title **Music to Grow Plants**

Dr Milstein certainly enjoys his plants. When not getting it on in the greenhouse, he was developing this special record to help the plants grow. It was kind of a vegetable Viagra. What he did with these swollen plants while alone in his greenhouse, we'll never know.

artist **VARIOUS ARTISTS**
title **Music for Bathroom Baritones/Bathing Beauties**

So, you're a plumbing company and you want to put out a record to give to your customers. Everyone else is doing it! But what to call your foray into vinyl? *Sounds of the Water Closet*? *A Century of Great Flushes*? I guess this will have to do – as long as you have a record player in the bathroom.

artist **THE DULUTH ACCORDIONAIRES**
title **Music to Eat Pizza By**

With the advent of frozen ready-meals, Americans could now enjoy their choice of cardboard 'n' cheese pizza in the privacy of their own home. Instead of listening to some washed-up Italian crooner, you can enhance your dinner with the sounds of school kids playing accordions.

music to soothe that tiger

DECCA RECORDS

HERBERT REHBEIN
AND HIS ORCHESTRA

Including:
WHEN I FALL IN LOVE
EAST OF THE SUN
CHANCES ARE
THE LADY SMILES
PRISONER OF LOVE
LOVE IS HERE TO STAY
IF I HAD YOU
SPEAK LOW

DL 4584

artist **HERBERT REHBEIN**
title **Music to Soothe That Tiger**

Nothing is sexier than a scantily clad woman sprawled out on the carcass of a dead animal. If you can't afford to smuggle in an endangered species, there are probably enough strays in your neighborhood to make a puppy rug at least.

JAY WILBUR & HIS STRING ORCHESTRA

music to love by

33⅓ RPM LONG PLAYING
L1507-149

TOPS
ULTRA-PHONIC SOUND / HIGH FIDELITY RECORDING

HOLIDAY FOR STRINGS
THE TOUCH OF YOUR LIPS
MAKE BELIEVE
ONE NIGHT OF LOVE
THESE FOOLISH THINGS
THEY DIDN'T BELIEVE ME
I'M GETTING SENTIMENTAL OVER YOU
THE VERY THOUGHT OF YOU
SUMMERTIME
LADY BE GOOD
TICO TICO
MAMSELLE

artist **JAY WILBUR & HIS STRING ORCHESTRA**
title **Music to Love By**

Here's a record that is sure to melt the heart of even the crankiest housewife. When husband comes home from a long day on the golf course, all he needs to do is drop the needle on this baby and the little lady will drop her mop and come running.

STEREO

MUSIC TO PAINT BY

ED AMES
What Color Is A Man

SERGIO FRANCHI
Blue Moon

JOHN GARY
Yellow Bird

SKITCH HENDERSON
Mood Indigo

LENA HORNE
Polka Dots And Moonbeams

THE NORMAN LUBOFF CHOIR
Ruby

TONY MARTIN
Green Eyes

PETER NERO
Over The Rainbow

DELLA REESE
Blue Skies

JIM REEVES
Scarlet Ribbons

artist **VARIOUS ARTISTS**
title **Music to Paint By**

The designers of this cover were tasked with 'sexing up' this paint record. They've done an admirable job. A pretty young couple covering the walls of their first home a rather startling shade of crimson, lost in a moment of painter's passion. 'Um, honey? My brush is getting stiff.'

artist   **GUCKENHEIMER SOUR KRAUT BAND**
title   **Music for Non Thinkers**

Some music requires entirely too much thought. The subtleties of a Puccini opera or a Mozart concerto require more brain power than many listeners want to provide. And while 'modern jazz' musicians were actively trying to scramble your grey matter, these fellows provided a vary happy medium.

10

Awfully Nice People

This chapter is about 'nice' singers. Mostly home-grown Christian artists, these Ned Flanders-types are the perfect next-door neighbor. They'll loan you their lawnmower when you're home, and collect your mail when you're away. As long as you're not up too late or decide to paint your house black, they'll be great.

There are the ladies – always smartly dressed in the latest home-made fashion, voluminously coiffed and usually carrying a freshly-cut rose. There are husband and wife teams, smiling and still very much in love, the husband often dwarfed by his wife's hair. Entire nice families may also be found, any hint of strife neatly packed away and forgotten. Nothing seems to get these folks down!

artist **CYNTHIA CLAWSON**
title **You're Welcome Here**

A popular Eighties hairstyle, the 'hair helmet' can still occasionally be seen, usually at weddings, receptions and other occasions, which call for a special 'do. I hope that's the case here – I'd hate to think Cynthia sets out the dinner table like this every day.

artist **BETH HOLLIS**
title **Until Sunrise**

'Until sunrise' seems to describe how long Ms Hollis stays out of doors. Lose the doily and get some sun, girl! She's just waiting for a sexy surfer to come and sweep her off her feet. Everyone knows the best waves are at sunrise. Hang ten, Beth!

artist **JOYCE**
title **Joyce**

Much has been written on the Internet about the enigmatic Joyce. She seems to have captured both the look and spirit of Tootsie like no one else. To me, she seems to be saying, 'Don't be afraid. Let's get together for a cup of coffee before my next hair appointment.'

110 • AWFULLY NICE PEOPLE

Now Let Me Sing

R-5009-LPS
Stereo

Lu Lu Roman
WITH THE BOB CLINE SINGERS

artist **LULU ROMAN**
title **Now Let Me Sing**

LuLu Roman, star of the *Hee Haw* televison show, reveals her 'outdoorsey' side. When not lounging around in the forest, she has recently written a cookbook and has a line of gourmet snacks called *LuLu Roman's Parlor Treats*.

artist **JUNE SMITHWICK**
title **Look To The Good Side**

Here's another lady-next-door who you can invite along on your coffee date with Joyce. They're even on the same record label! Perhaps they have some sort of 'I'm nicer than you' rivalry that might spill over into a battle of empty smiles and icy glares. Let's keep it civil now, ladies!

112 • AWFULLY NICE PEOPLE

artist **JACQUE**
title **Jacque**
What an important moment it is when an artist makes that creative leap of faith and decides to go by one name only. Jacque chooses this eyeball-bending glitzy shot to capture that moment forever.

artist **THE NORTHAMS**
title **Come On Down**
These folks look like a group of my high school teachers dressed up for the end-of-the-year ice cream social. On the right? She taught art class and even made the little shell necklaces! The tall guy? Maths teacher, but a hairstylist on the weekend.

114 • AWFULLY NICE PEOPLE

THE BRAILLETTES
Our Hearts Keep Singing

Heart Warming Records
HWS 1998 STEREO

His Smile
The Innkeeper
How Rich I Am
Tenderly He Calls
This Is My Prayer
He'll Never Let You Fall
All Day Long My Heart Keeps Singing
The First Thing I Do Every Morning
That's What He Did For Me
Will He Know Me?
Soon It Is Over

artist **THE BRAILLETTES**
title **Our Hearts Keep Singing**

This is truly a unique album cover that manages to be shocking, funny and kind of cute all at the same time! Jackie, Maggie and Kay were three young blind singers from California, who brought their special vision to the 'spiritually blind'.

Sing Live Again

AWFULLY NICE PEOPLE • 115

artist **WALLY AND GINGER**
title **Sing Live Again**
Well this one just makes me giggle. Wally and Ginger had a funny idea for their album cover and by golly no-one was going to talk them out of it. Their stage performances were probably quite lively and fun, even if the palette of their costume department didn't extend much beyond 'brown'.

artist **THE MCDONALD SISTERS**
title **I've Got Confidence**

It's a strange method of confidence building. Dressing your awkward teenage children in horrible home-made outfits and pasting their picture on an album cover for all eternity does not seem to be the best method. We all have childhood pictures like this – most of us keep them hidden!

Lost In His Love

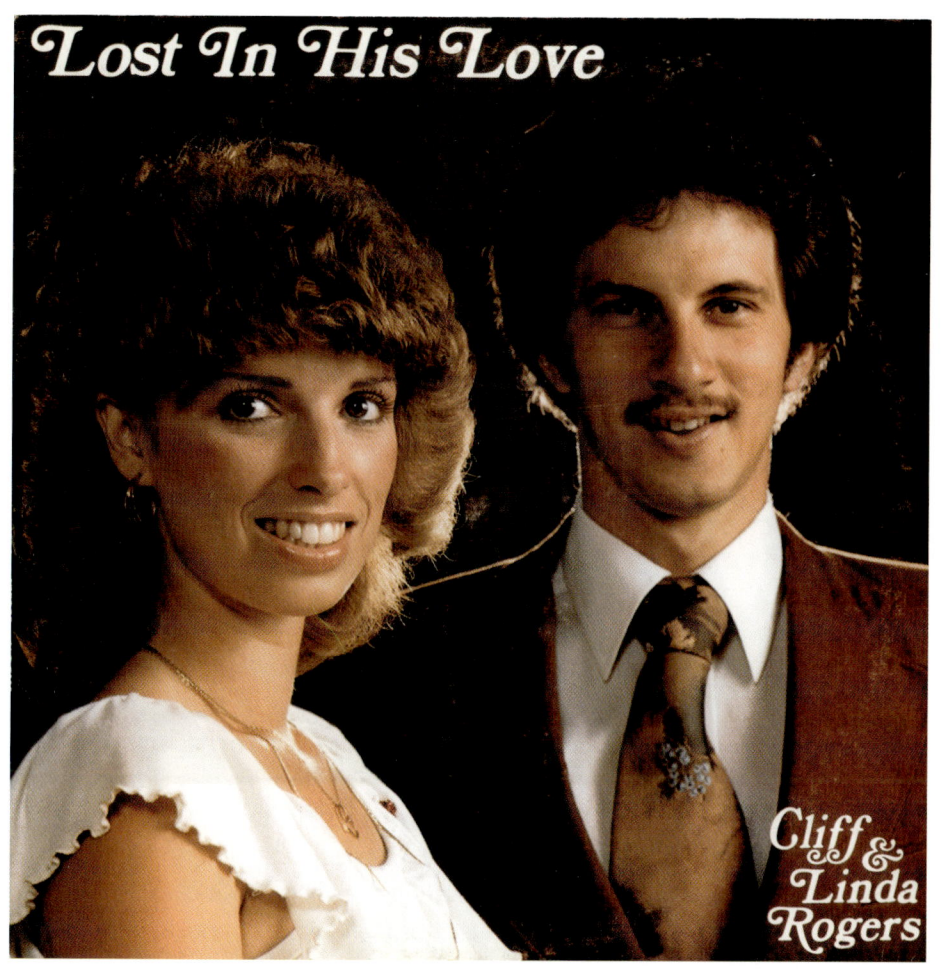

artist **CLIFF & LINDA ROGERS**
title **Lost In His Love**

The sky's the limit for this glamorous pair. Performing in small-town Kansas is but a stepping stone to the clubs of Manhattan and the salons of Paris. In the days before *American Idol*, you had only to put out a record and wait for your big break!

11

Never Too Old

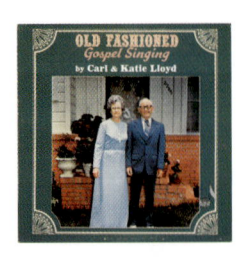

It is always refreshing to see people with a few rings on the tree stump throw aside their walkers and make a record. Older artists perform for different reasons than their younger counterparts. Some have spent their whole lives working the day job, neglecting their artistic side as a result, and finally, in one great spurt of creativity before Old Man Reaper comes a-calling, the opportunity arises to leave their artistic mark on the world.

Older performers also have different priorities. No sex, drugs and rock 'n' roll here, more like sleep, medication and funeral arrangements. Thus, if you want to see older performers playing a young man's game, you can either pay $200 for Rolling Stones tickets or take a look at the records in this chapter.

artist **THE EIGHT BALLS**
title **A Musical Essay on Dixieland Jazz**

Boy, these guys are a real riot. I can imagine that the old 'pop out of the casket' trick goes down really well at funerals. I wonder why they chose the youngest fellow to be the one in the casket? Probably some sort of initiation ritual. Having only been in the band for 20 years, he's still the new guy.

Music Boxes and Chiming Clocks from the

Alec Templeton
Collection

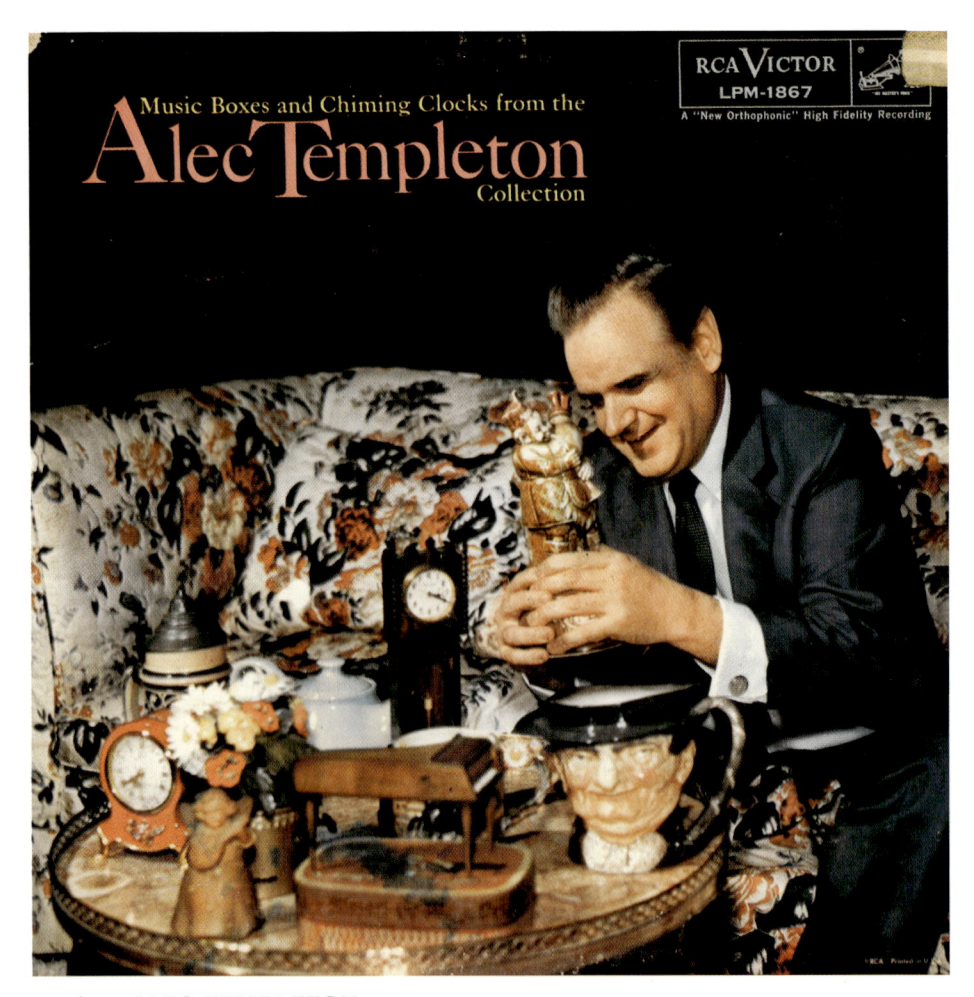

RCA VICTOR
LPM-1867
A "New Orthophonic" High Fidelity Recording

120 • NEVER TOO OLD

artist **ALEC TEMPLETON**
title   **Music Boxes and Chiming Clocks**

Mr Templeton is obviously very fond of his collection. 'Yesssss, my pretties!' For him, putting out this record was probably a bit like how I feel about writing this book: finally, my collection of junk is paying off! Really, though, I don't think I'll be listening to this one any time soon.

artist **THE MINISTERS QUARTET**
title **Let Me Touch Him**

Even without the ominous title, this creepy looking quartet is enough to have the children hiding in the bushes as they go by. I suppose we should give these guys some credit — at least they're *asking* this time.

artist **CARL & KATIE LLOYD**
title **Old Fashioned Gospel Singing**

Imagine living next to the Lloyds. Constantly up all night, partying with their band buddies, raising a ruckus and keeping the whole street awake. Marathon jamming sessions at all hours are weekly occurrences, and who knows what they're smoking back in the shed.

artist **MRS. MILLS**
title **Knees-Up Party**

A party just isn't a party until your grandmother starts singing. Usually that doesn't happen until she's polished off quite a few pints. That's perhaps why, as a general rule, you never see pubs in retirement homes – you never know what kind of crazy things the old dears might get up to!

artist **CARROLL ATCHISON**
title **Come To The Chapel**

When trying to encourage young children to attend church, it is probably not the best idea to put such a nightmare-inducing couple on the cover. This ghastly photograph would be better used on a horror movie poster. 'Yes, children, come to the Chapel… of Doom!'

Songs That Mom and Dad Taught Us

THE FRIENDS

STEREO   STEREO

NEVER TOO OLD • 125

artist **THE FRIENDS**
title **Songs That Mom and Dad Taught Us**
Ah, memories of Mom and Dad... The squeak of polyester on vinyl flooring, the smell of mothballs and stale cigar smoke, the conch shell hidden under the television. Don't worry, a quick trip to IKEA and all their decorating problems will be solved.

12

Organ Fascination

In the heyday of vinyl, virtually every instrument had its day. There were banjo records, marimba records, harmonica records and accordion records.

But by far the biggest sub-genre of instrument novelties was the organ record. It seems everybody had an organ and those who didn't wanted one – call it 'organ envy'. And really, the organ is a strange instrument to receive such adulation. The guitar has always been cool. The drums? Well, we all know what drummers are like. Woodwinds are whack and brass is bogus. Even the boring old piano tried to get in on the act, as shown by a few covers here. But there is no denying, the organ is where it's at.

artist **DAVE STEPHENS**
title **Organ Fascination**

Most organ records have a subtle sexual subtext — you just have to look a bit. This one doesn't even bother showing the keyboard! This woman has finally realized that, once you play the organ, it's tough to go back to playing the piano.

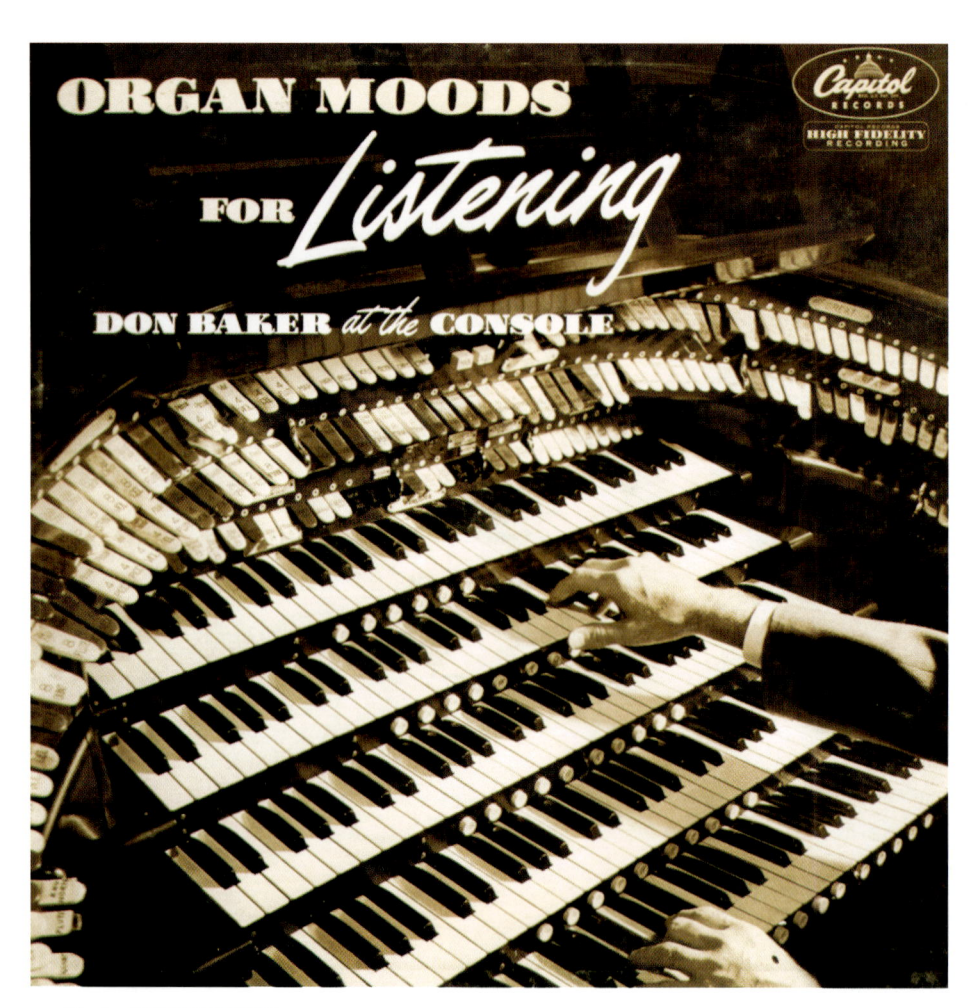

ORGAN MOODS FOR Listening
DON BAKER at the CONSOLE

artist **DON BAKER**
title **Organ Moods for Listening**

Whoever said that size isn't everything obviously didn't play the organ in the golden age of vinyl. To be successful, you did need a big organ – one with lots of keys, buttons, bells and whistles. It must have been frustrating for the musicians, who rarely got their faces on the cover, but just their hands on their organ.

artist **KEN DEMKO**
title **Live at the Lamplighter Inn**

Here's a guy who managed to get some face time on his album cover. As he lovingly caresses the keys, he seems to acknowledge the fact that his organ may not be as big as some. But what do you expect at the Lamplighter Inn? Everyone knows all the best organs are in Vegas.

THE MIGHTIEST WURLITZER

EDDIE WEAVER AT THE CONSOLE

FULL SOUND STEREO

CONCERT RECORDING
CR-0019

artist **EDDIE WEAVER**
title **The Mightiest Wurlitzer**

Eddie Weaver is so proud of his organ, he made a shirt for it. It's like those people who put sweaters on their dogs. With his matching jacket, sometimes it's hard to tell where Eddie ends and the organ begins.

artist **JONATHAN EDWARDS**
title **The Piano Artistry of Jonathan Edwards**

What's so funny about this record? A rather modest set of keys, not even an organ, really. Why'd he put this thing in the book? Unless… Wait a minute… Let me take another look… I've heard of two left feet, but two right hands? No wonder she seems so excited about the night to come.

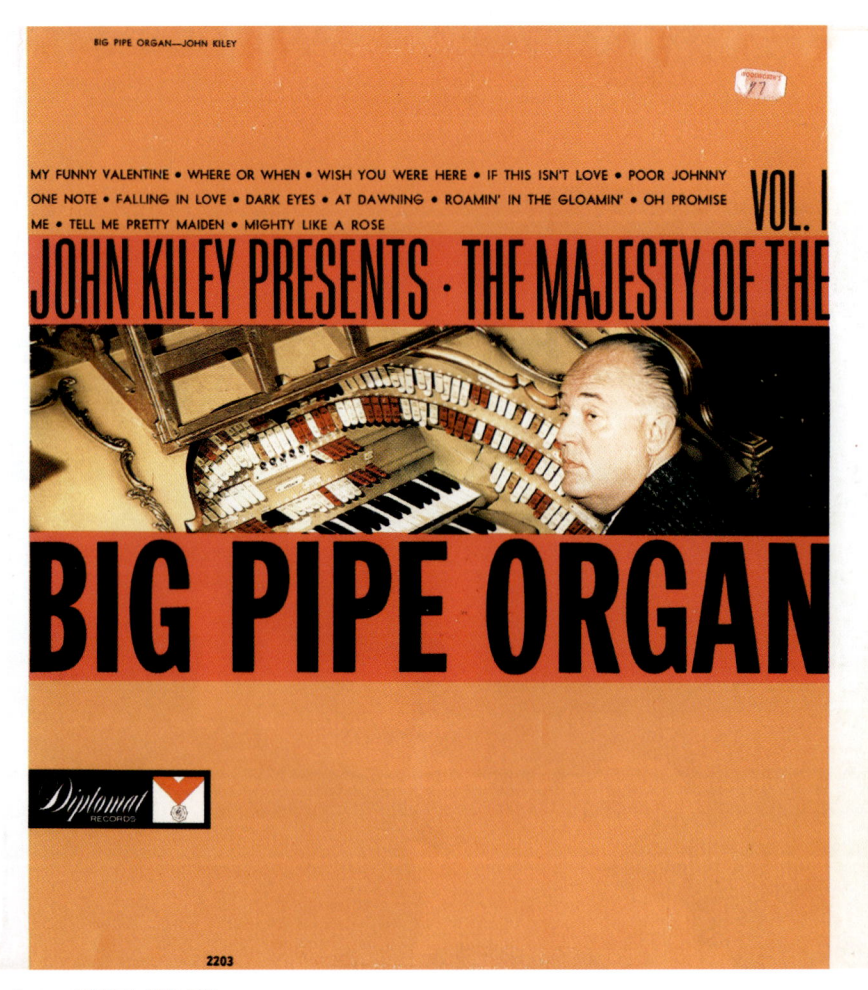

artist **JOHN KILEY**

title **The Majesty of the Big Pipe Organ**

Mr Kiley doesn't look too happy to have his picture taken. Apparently he doesn't like to be interrupted. His organ is so big, we can only be shown a small part of it. If you want to see the whole thing, you'll have to see Mr Kiley in person.

ORGAN FASCINATION • 133

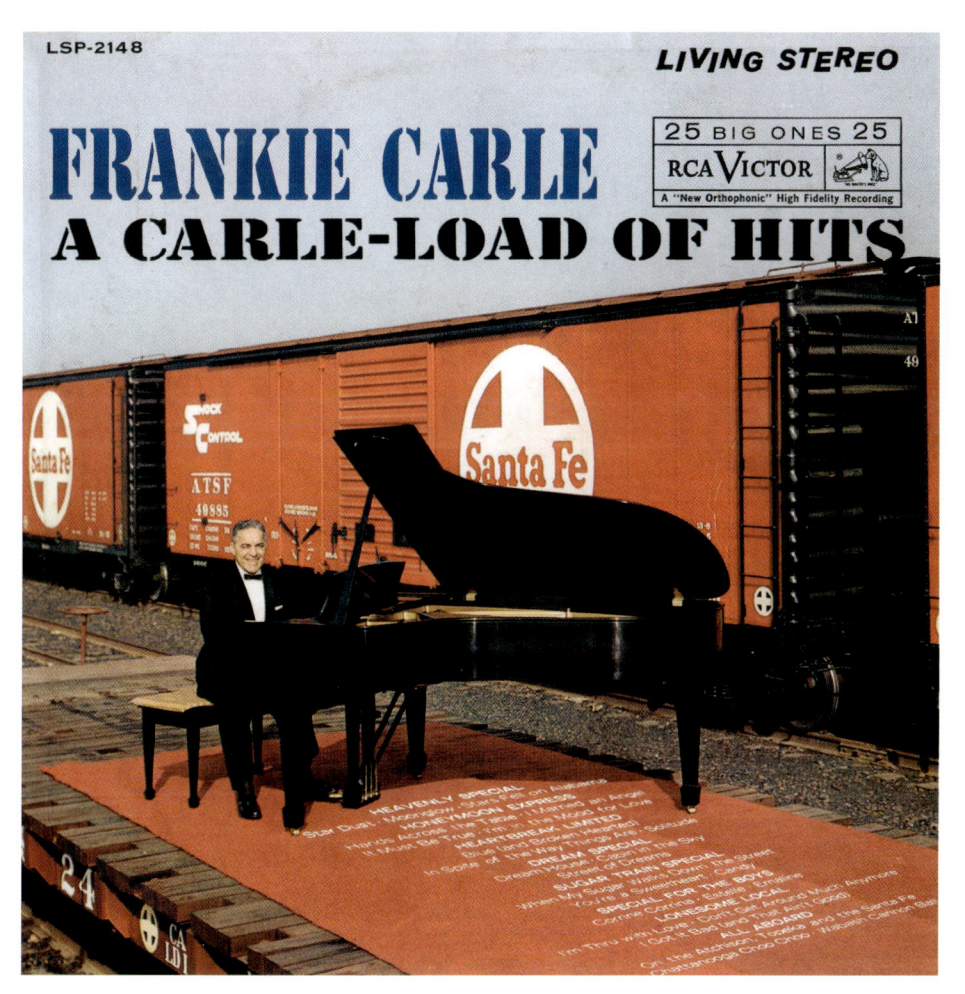

artist **FRANKIE CARLE**
title **A Carle-Load of Hits**

The organ guys had competition from piano men like Frankie. Compared to the room-sized pipe organs, Carle's instrument seems almost portable. All he needs is his own private train carriage and he can go on a world tour!

ORGAN MOODS IN HI-FI

CUSTOM HIGH FIDELITY
Mercury MG 20208

featuring eddie layton

artist **EDDIE LAYTON**
title **Organ Moods in Hi-Fi**

Eddie Layton thoroughly enjoys both his organ and his microphone. That wouldn't be so strange except for the fact that Eddie doesn't even sing! Perhaps because his organ is so small, the photographer thought he had to liven things up a bit.

artist **THE MUSTANG**
title **Organ Freakout!**

As the 1960s progressed, tastes changed. Big pipe organs were for the old fogies, but new, portable machines meant that instead of the party coming to the organ, the organ could come to the party! All you need is a gang of loose women in tight clothes… Let the freakout begin!

13

Polka Party

Polka music is fun, goofy and a bit strange, and the album covers show it. This is party music for the young at heart.

Legend has it that the Polka dance was invented by a Czech peasant girl in 1834. The dance soon swept Europe and arrived in America. The craze spawned such inventions as polka hats, polka ties and polka dots, though only the dots and the music have stuck around.

Polka music may be thought uncool by some, but the Polka people don't care. They're having so much fun, they'll tell you to grab a beer and join in!

artist **VERNON BELIK**
title **For All My Friends**

Vernon has lots of friends. They always promise they're going to show up to his gigs, but for some reason they never seem to make it. No worries. With this record, they now have no excuse not to listen to Vernon and his squeeze-box in all their ear-splitting glory!

OH YEAH! IT'S PAYDAY AT A POLKA PARTY

THE COAL DIGGERS with HAPPY TONY

THE GREATEST POLKAS EVER PUT ON RECORDS!!
RECORDED LIVE WITH A DANCING AND SINGING AUDIENCE!!

artist **THE COAL DIGGERS WITH HAPPY TONY**
title **Oh Yeah! It's Payday at a Polka Party**

You have never really been to a party until you've been to a coal-miners' polka party. Having never been, I'll have to guess what its like. Lots of drinking, dancing and black lung for all? Just don't request 'The Roof is On Fire'… They don't find that joke funny.

artist **HAPPY LOUIE, JULCIA AND THE BOYS**
title **Lots of Love & Peace**

Polka bands are always trying to hop on the latest youth trends. The brief period of 'hippy polka' was exemplified by this lovely record. The boys grew their hair out for days to get this look. They tried to get on the bill at Woodstock, but were unfortunately bumped for Sha-Na-Na.

artist **THE H.O.T. CZECHS**
title **Goin' Bankin'**

When the Hot Czechs needed a loan to get their tuxedos pressed and the Winnebago back on the road, they had to look no further than the local bank. Perhaps they should team up with the local garage, so they can get a cheap tow when the thing breaks down.

MY POLISH GIRLFRIEND

by the **POLKA SHARPS of LORAIN, OHIO**

JR-LP1001

POLKA PARTY • 141

artist   **THE POLKA SHARPS**
title   **My Polish Girlfriend**

Well, you know what they say about Polish girls, don't you? Okay, neither do I. Of course making a record with your girlfriend's picture on it doesn't seem like the best idea. Slightly better than getting her name tattooed on your arm, but not much.

artist **WALTER SOLEK AND HIS ORCHESTRA**
title **40 20 35 Polka**

This polka hottie shows off the perfect polka measurements. I don't imagine that most female polka fans fit the bill quite so well, but once the accordions are playing and the beer is flowing, who's going to notice, anyway?

artist **STANKY & HIS COAL MINERS POLKA BAND**
title **Now Coal Mines are Closing Polka**

Polka bands seem to know how to make the best of a good thing. Making a lump of coal into a diamond, if you will. Here, though Stanky has lost his job, he now finds more time to serenade the ladies above ground. His next single is likely to be the *Now Wal-Mart is Hiring Polka*.

14

Rockers

The first big album cover controversy concerned the now-infamous 'butcher cover' from the Beatles 1966 US release, *Yesterday, Today and Tomorrow*. This mind-bogglingly tasteless cover shows the boys yukking it up in butchers' smocks, covered in baby doll parts and bloody cuts of meat. Within days the cover was recalled, and original copies have become one of the most treasured rock 'n' roll collectibles.

And so, we see that even the biggest names in music and the most deeply-pocketed record companies can produce an amazingly horrible album cover. What hope for the average rocker-on-the-street?

artist **HELLO PEOPLE**
title **Bricks**

These are not the mime artists you'd want to meet in a dark alley late at night. They're likely to beat you with invisible clubs and take your imaginary wallet. Maybe you can get some help from the clowns around the corner, who can assault them with a battery of very real rubber chickens.

artist **CERRONE 3**
title **Supernature**

Operating table with anatomical dummy? Check. Crawling pig man and two other unidentifiable beasts? Check. Strange man with disco shirt and chain? Check. Most incomprehensible album cover ever? You be the judge.

artist **FURR**
title **Furr**

It looks to me as if these guys really wanted to look like Kiss, but couldn't afford the outfits. Fortunately, somebody was nearby with an airbrush and a vivid imagination. Perhaps with a prayer to the spandex gods, their fondest costume dreams will become a reality.

148 • ROCKERS

artist **MAD MAX**
title **Rollin' Thunder**
These hard rocking boys have more leather than a football factory. Like many of their heavy metal counterparts, their look shares as much with S&M as it does with rock 'n' roll.

artist **RED ROCKERS**
title **Schizophrenic Circus**
Surprisingly, this cover was not designed by Salvador Dali or Fedirico Fellini. Whoever it was, they should be forever barred from coming near an album cover ever again. Bands: when someone says, 'Don't you think this would be a great cover?' sometimes it's better to just say, 'No'.

artist **THOR**
title **Keep The Dogs Away**

Thor – just your average, everyday body builder/dog walker/heavy metal singer. Every street has one! He's easy to buy a present for – a big jar of cocoa butter and a bag of dog biscuits and he's happy. Lock up your kittens!

ROCKERS • 151

artist **VARIOUS ARTISTS**
title **All Day Thumb Sucker**
I don't know much about art but I know what not to sit on! I really don't know what's going on with this cover. It seems to be another attempt at being shocking through sheer nonsense. Or maybe they just needed a quick cover photo and this giant hand was out in the trash.

15

Saved Men

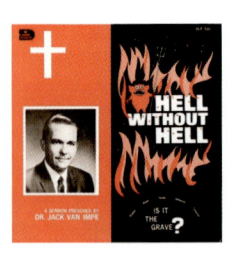

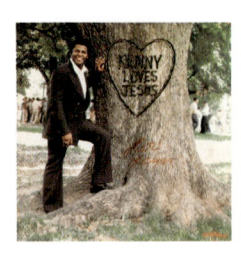

The saved man: some are preachers, professionals if you will. They not only have their ticket to Heaven, but are doing their best to get you on board too. Some have huge budgets and national TV audiences to support their soul-saving habit, while small-time, local reverends have to get creative if they want to keep the pews full. Some saved men use another gimmick to attract fans to their church performances: their own disabilities. Though shocking at first, they are hardly the first performers to get by on their looks. Some saved men are simply men whose singing talent is too large to be kept in church. They have to make a record, too.

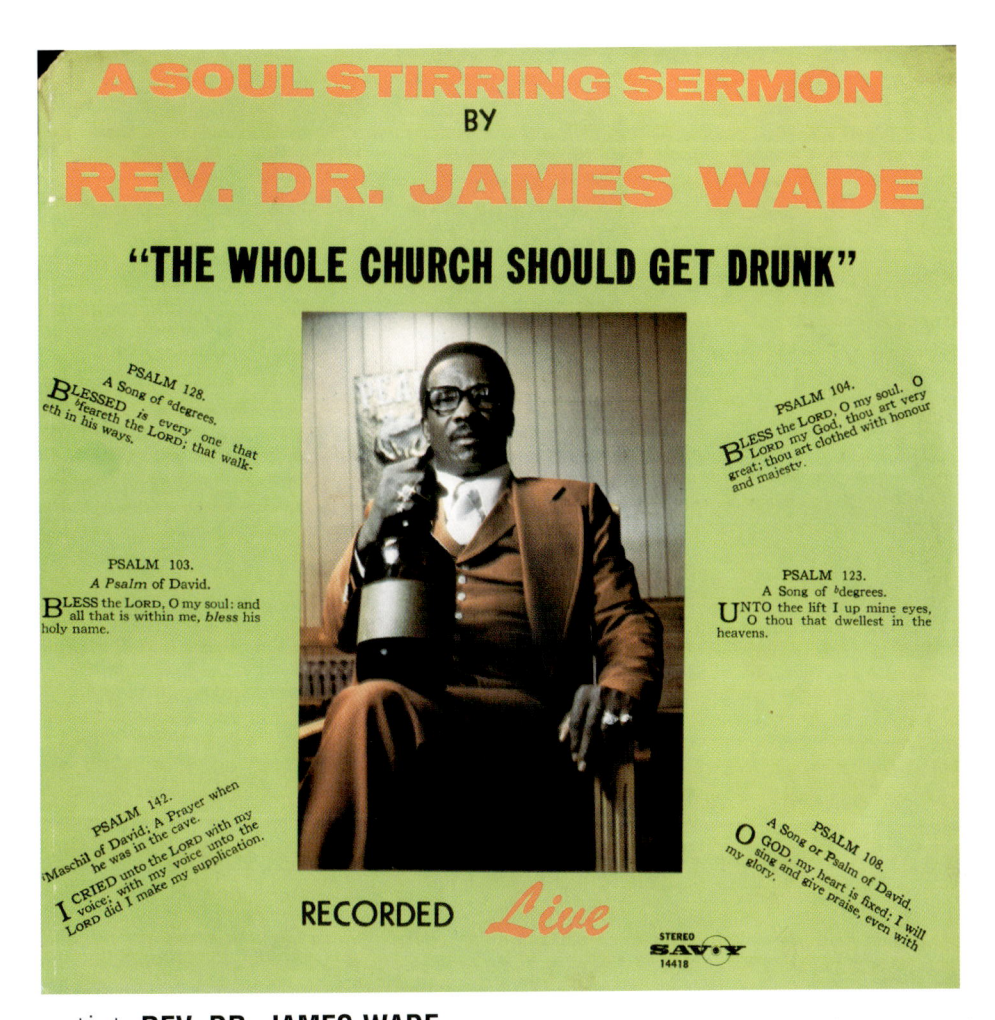

artist   **REV. DR. JAMES WADE**
title   **The Whole Church Should Get Drunk**

Preachers… Always a wet blanket at a party. Do this. Don't do that. Don't cuss. Give money to the poor. It's enough to put a man off church for good. But at last, here's a guy who knows how to really get the congregation jumping – he'll soon find he has the most popular church in town!

BEFORE *"Nature Boy"* **TOMMY PHELPS**

R-2045 LPD

I WRESTLED WITH GOD!

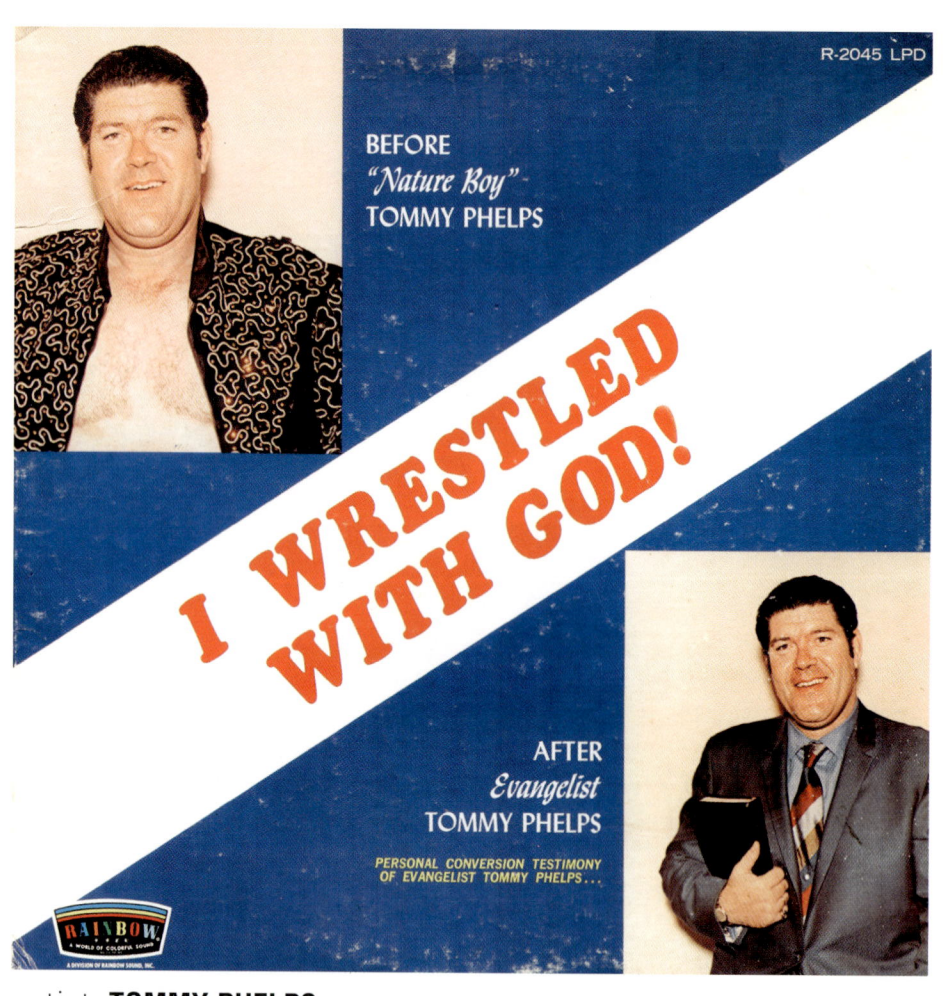

AFTER *Evangelist* **TOMMY PHELPS**

PERSONAL CONVERSION TESTIMONY OF EVANGELIST TOMMY PHELPS...

artist **TOMMY PHELPS**
title **I Wrestled With God!**

Most of these born-again Christian preachers came from a life of crime, sin, and debauchery. Tommy Phelps was a professional wrestler. Sometimes, he didn't even button his shirt. Compare the 'before' and 'after' shots… It looks like they were taken five minutes apart!

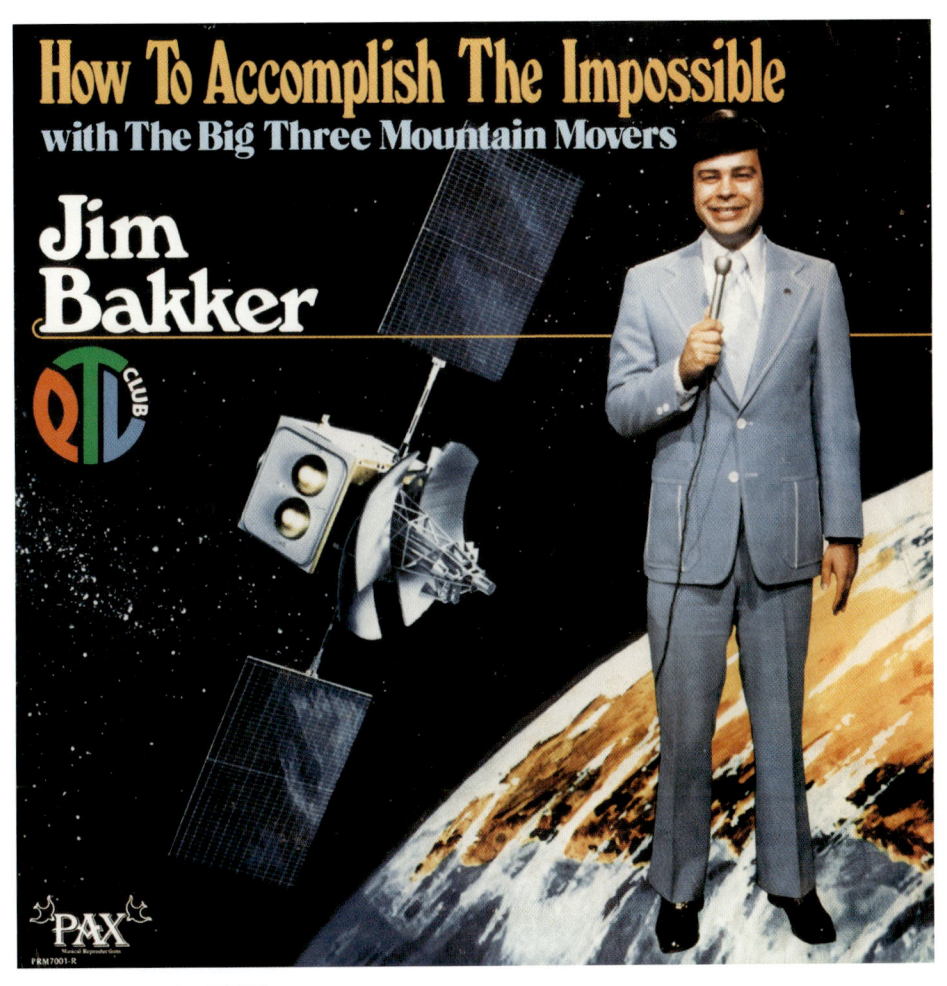

artist **JIM BAKKER**
title **How To Accomplish the Impossible**

Jim Bakker surely knew how to move mountains, build gigantic churches, and launch satellites. When wife Tammy Faye wasn't hogging the spotlight, Jim was busy giving NASA a run for their money with his satellite television network. His space suit, however, needs improvement.

156 • SAVED MEN

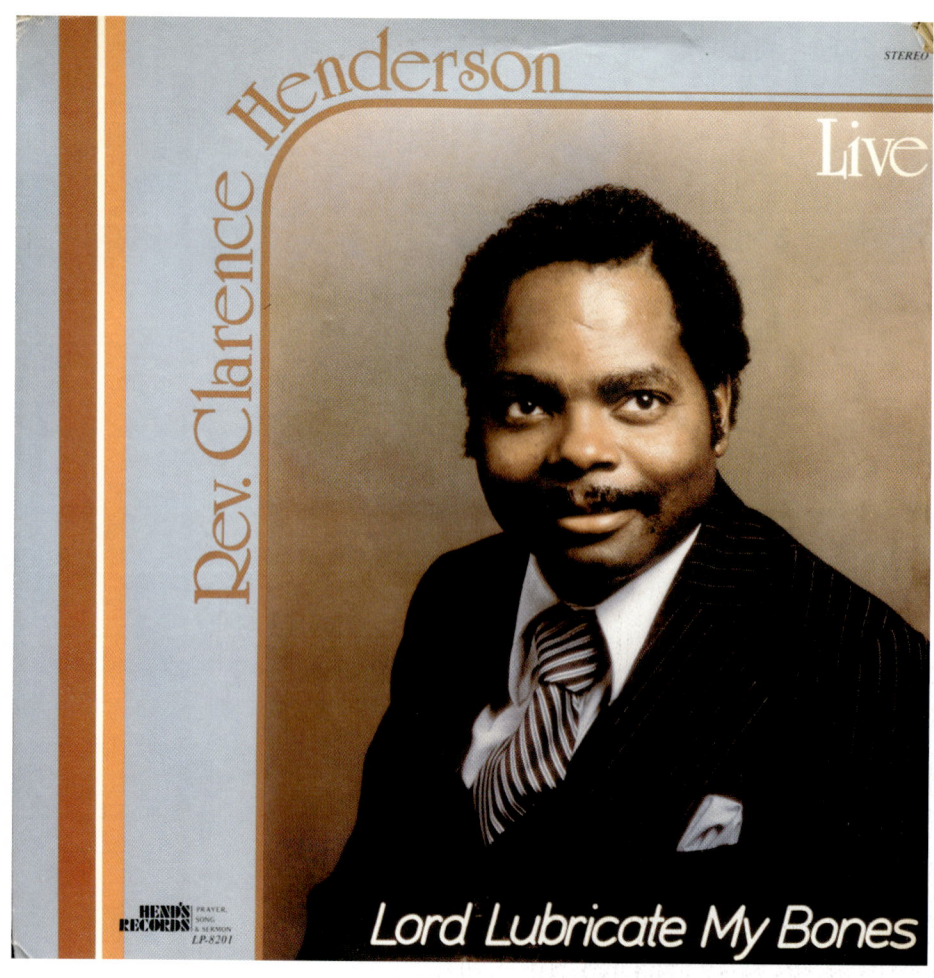

REV. CLARENCE HENDERSON
Live
STEREO
HEND'S RECORDS PRAYER, SONG & SERMON LP-8201
Lord Lubricate My Bones

artist **REV. CLARENCE HENDERSON**
title **Lord Lubricate My Bones**
Is this a sermon for zombie skeletons or something? Or perhaps he's planning on getting together with Rev. Wade for a little lubrication from the bottle. Whatever the case, it's great that Rev. Henderson managed to get his bones oiled enough to make this record.

SOMETHING SPECIAL from *Jeff*

Featuring: Through it All

STEREO
HPS 7739

artist **JEFF**
title **Something Special**
Jeff is one of those bold fellows who never let his many disabilities get in the way of a career on stage. Really, when a guy shows up with deformed legs and a hook hand, it's probably best just to let him do what he wants. Jeff also has a comedy tape about being drafted into the military.

158 • SAVED MEN

STEREO

DOYLE JONES

I've Had A Touch From The Lord

LEFEVRE SOUND
2720

artist   **DOYLE JONES**
title   **I've Had A Touch From The Lord**

Like many other 'Saved Men', Doyle has seen the light. But has he been touched by the Lord or just touched in the head? Whatever the case, I just hope he's been touched in the vocal cords – I've heard enough terrible singing while writing this book!

merrill womach
happy again

featuring the song "Happy Again" as sung in the award winning Mel White color motion picture, "HE RESTORETH MY SOUL"

stereo

SAVED MEN • 159

artist **MERRILL WOMACH**
title **Happy Again**

Merrill Womach was already a gospel singer when a horrific airplane crash nearly ended his life, but it took years of rehabilitation, medicine, and botched plastic surgery to make him a star. Oh sure, you can laugh, but are the stretched and Botoxed faces of modern celebrities any worse?

GLENDA LEE (DAY) and RICHARD MILLER
special: DIXIE ECHOES ('66)

artist   **GLENDA LEE (DAY) AND RICHARD MILLER**
title   **Special: Dixie Echoes ('66)**

As we have seen, many 'physically challenged' artists have put out records. Few, however, are as challenged as Mr Miller. If nothing else, the fact that this guy can play the guitar is testament to the strength of the human will to succeed.

artist **KENNY RODGERS**
title **Kenny Loves Jesus**

Kenny, Kenny, Kenny.... We know you love Jesus, but do you have to deface public property to tell us? Couldn't you just put a sign up in your garden or perhaps just put a sticker on your bumper?

162 • SAVED MEN

artist **DR. JACK VAN IMPE**
title **Hell Without Hell - Is It The Grave?**

Dr Van Impe has been preaching gloom and doom for 50-odd years. By scaring the wits out of his followers, in this case with evil little cartoon characters, the good doctor has proven one thing: if at first you don't succeed at bringing the world to an end, try, try again.

A comprehensive message delivered by Dr. Jerry Falwell, pastor, Thomas Road Baptist Church, Lynchburg, Va., which clearly answers man's most puzzling question.

The beautiful special music is provided by Doug Oldham and the Old-Time Gospel Hour choir.

Where are the Dead?

artist **DR. JERRY FALWELL**
title **Where Are the Dead?**

Here's another charming fellow who is all too happy to remind you of your impending demise. You're going to die soon. Surely you don't need all that money you're hiding away? Why not make things easy on yourself and send your life savings to me?

16

Bad Girls

Sex sells and record cover designers have known it since the early days. So-called 'cheesecake' covers were the usual fare for many top selling records in the 1950s and 1960s. Many of these covers are quite beautiful and stand out as great examples of the album cover design genre. But you didn't expect to find those in this book, did you?

In this chapter you'll find some examples that are a bit more strange. A few are attempts at cheesecake covers that didn't quite come off, while others simply show the artist lost in her own sexy world.

artist **ELKIE BROOKS**
title **Rich Man's Woman**

I have no idea what prompted Ms. Brooks to photograph her naked electro-shock therapy session and use it for an album cover. I suppose that some people are proud of their armpits and others aren't.

166 • BAD GIRLS

artist **JACKIE GLEASON**
title **Music to Remember Her**

The 1950s was a truly swinging time. The women were so loose you needed an entire record album to remember them all. I suppose that's better than collecting their disembodied heads. But what happened when you met a lady who didn't have a song named after her?

artist **THE SPORTSMEN QUARTET**
title **Barbershop Ballads**

No explanation is offered as to why this busty babe is lounging at the barbershop. Perhaps she just likes barber poles? The quartet seems to be having enough trouble keeping each of theirs under control.

168 • BAD GIRLS

I'm in the mood for the Magic Trumpet of Billy Butterfield and his orchestra

artist **BILLY BUTTERFIELD AND HIS ORCHESTRA**
title **I'm in the mood**

I think this record was probably marketed toward a female audience. After a hard day of housework, most women did not want to waste time with pleasantries when her man finally got home from work. Just pop this baby on the turntable and her husband instantly knows what's expected of him.

Music for a STRIP TEASE PARTY

A HOME TERTAINMENT PROGRAM with THE FUN BEAT!

"BALD" BILL HAGAN and His TROCADERONS

artist   **"BALD" BILL HAGAN AND HIS TROCADERONS**
title   **Music for a Strip Tease Party**

A strip tease party requires music all its own, as anyone knows who's ever tried it using their Led Zeppelin records. Really, it's all about the 'fun beat'. The lady may want to practise a bit with the guys from the office before trying it out on her special man.

artist **MILLIE JACKSON**
title **Back to the S__t!**

Mille Jackson is known for her strange, risqué album covers, but this one takes the cake and runs away with the spoon. Can you imagine the looks in the record company boardroom when these photographs came in? Congratulations, Millie, you have my vote for the most tasteless album cover ever made!

artist **SYLVIA SMITH**
title **Woman of the World**

I'm not entirely sure what Sylvia has in her hands there, but for some reason it looks painful. She also seems to be wearing nothing under that fur coat apart from her shoes. She definitely has plans for somebody – I just hope it's not me!

STEREO
WARNER BROS
1400 • HIGH FIDELITY

HOW TO GET THE MOST OUT OF YOUR STEREO

MUSICAL SELECTIONS
SPECIALLY ENGINEERED
TO CHALLENGE EVERY
COMPONENT OF
YOUR STEREO
SYSTEM

"Warner Bros. widespread stereo... the finest on records"
— HIGH FIDELITY

artist **VARIOUS ARTISTS**
title **How To Get the Most Out Of Your Stereo**

These folks really knew how to sell a boring old hi-fi test record. Apparently, if your stereo is hooked up right, you will have the ability to send women into fits of ecstasy. I'm not really sure why this babe is wearing a stethoscope, but I've learned not to ask too many questions.

artist **BOBBI BAKER**
title **I'll Do Anything For Money!**

When a lady says to me, 'I'll do anything for money', my first thought generally does not involve elephants. But hey, when it's your money, you make the call. I can think of a lot worse requests than to play around with circus animals.

17

That's Just Silly

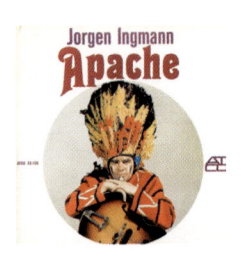

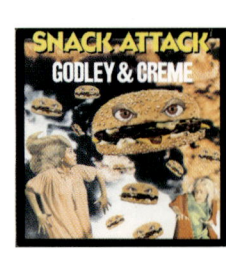

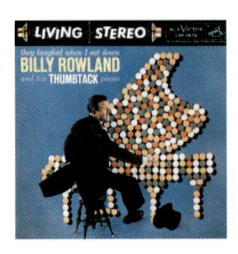

Sometimes a strange album cover is just plain good marketing – a designer knows that an odd image will catch the buyer's eye.

Unsurprisingly, comedy albums are the most commonly seen examples of silliness. When 'international concert comedienne' Anna Russell surrounds herself with menacing Afro-Hollywood natives for her cover or Frank Fontaine hams it up with his drunken cross-eyed face, you know the record is going to be hi-LAR-ious!

Musical artists often get in on the act, too, when all other album cover ideas fail. When the guy on the cover is blowing bubbles in a plastic chalice or playing a piano made of thumbtacks, who wouldn't plunk down a few dollars to hear what the darn record sounds like?

artist **RANDY VAN HORNE AND HIS SWINGING CHOIR**
title **Clef Dwellers**

Here's an album cover that shows the big labels can have cheap, tacky covers, too. I'm sure these models all thought that this would be their big break in to showbiz. But if climbing up a cardboard wall and sticking your head through a hole is what it takes to make it, then go for it!

JIM POST
I love my life

artist **JIM POST**
title **I Love My Life**
A refreshing woodland shower might be a nice change of pace. But one should beware. Not only are the local authorities likely to start getting concerned calls from local hikers, but if there's a bear attack, you don't want to get caught with your pants down.

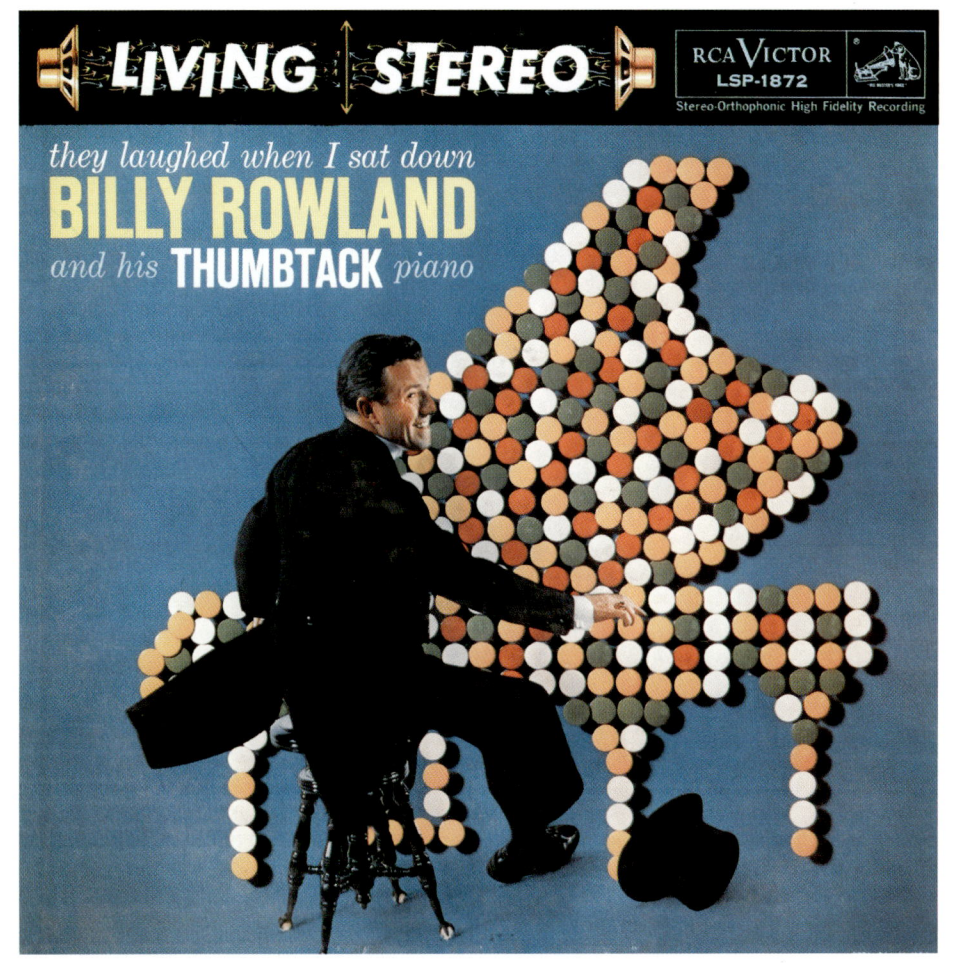

artist **BILLY ROWLAND AND HIS THUMBTACK PIANO**
title **They Laughed When I Sat Down**

Laugh at my thumbtacks, will you? Will you laugh when I land a major record deal? Will you laugh when I am playing in front of thousands of screaming fans, begging for me to toss them a spent tack? Will you laugh when I am in a book of bad album covers?

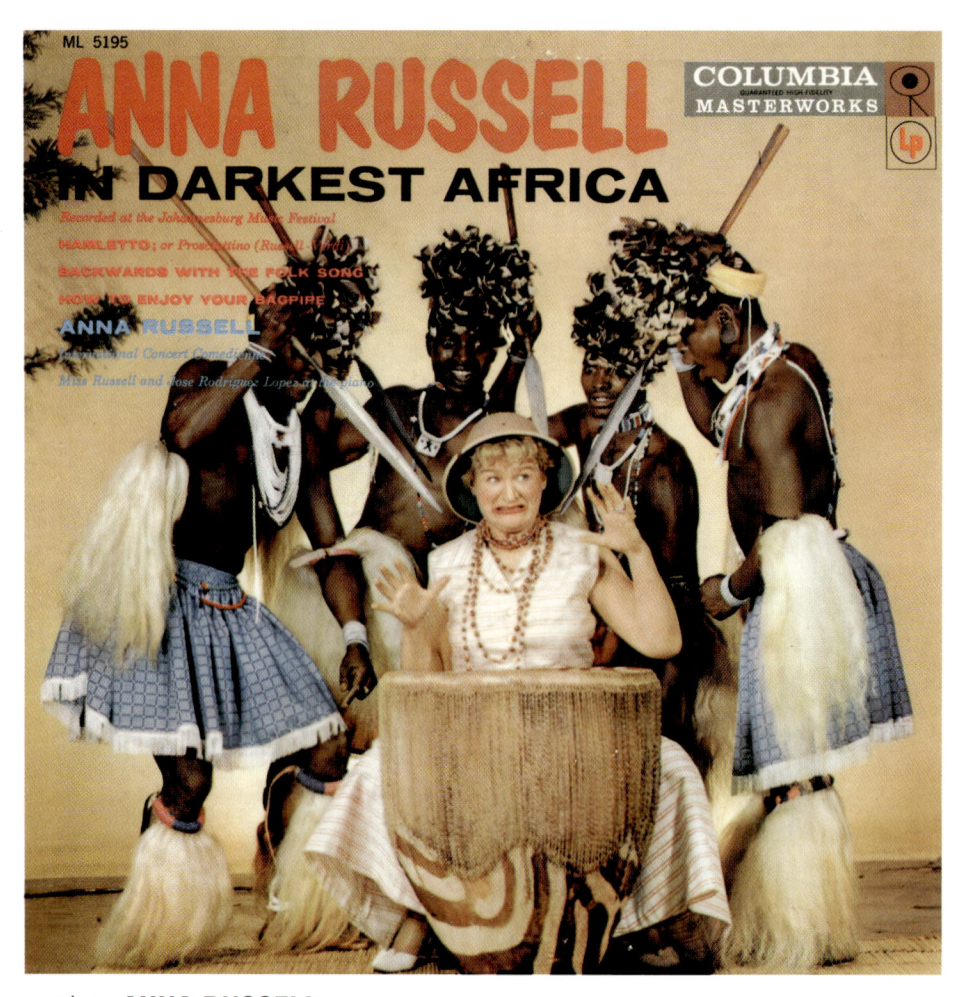

artist **ANNA RUSSELL**
title **In Darkest Africa**

This one is definitely an all-time classic bad album cover! The natives, clad in tablecloths and Pomeranian dogs, seem to be moments away from sending Ms Russell to the cooking pot on a skewer. I guess she shouldn't have messed with their drum!

artist **FRANK FONTAINE**
title **Songs I Sing on the Jackie Gleason Show**

Frank played the goofy, perpetually drunk Crazy Guggenheim character on the Jackie Gleason show. This record was actually a number one hit on the Billboard charts in 1962, which says more about the records people bought in 1962 than I care to think about.

artist **OSCAR BRAND**
title **Out of the Blue**

Here's another wacky singer with lots of wacky record cover ideas. Oscar scoured military bases for bawdy ballads and popularized lovely tunes such as 'Will You Go Boom Today?' and 'Every Inch a Sailor'.

artist **SHEP FIELDS**
title **Rippling Rhythm in Hi-Fi**

Plenty of talented musicians have mastered the guitar, the trumpet or the violin. Only one man has mastered the soda straw. Although he (sadly) doesn't actually play the straw on the record, Shep had a good gimmick, and he was not about to blow this opportunity at fame!

182 • THAT'S JUST SILLY

ATCO 33-130

Jorgen Ingmann
Apache

artist **JORGEN INGMANN**
title **Apache**

Everything about this record is authentic American Indian. Everything, that is, except the guitar. And the head-dress and tunic. And Jorgen Ingmann, who's from Denmark. And the songs, like 'Echo Boogie' and 'The March of the Siamese Children'.

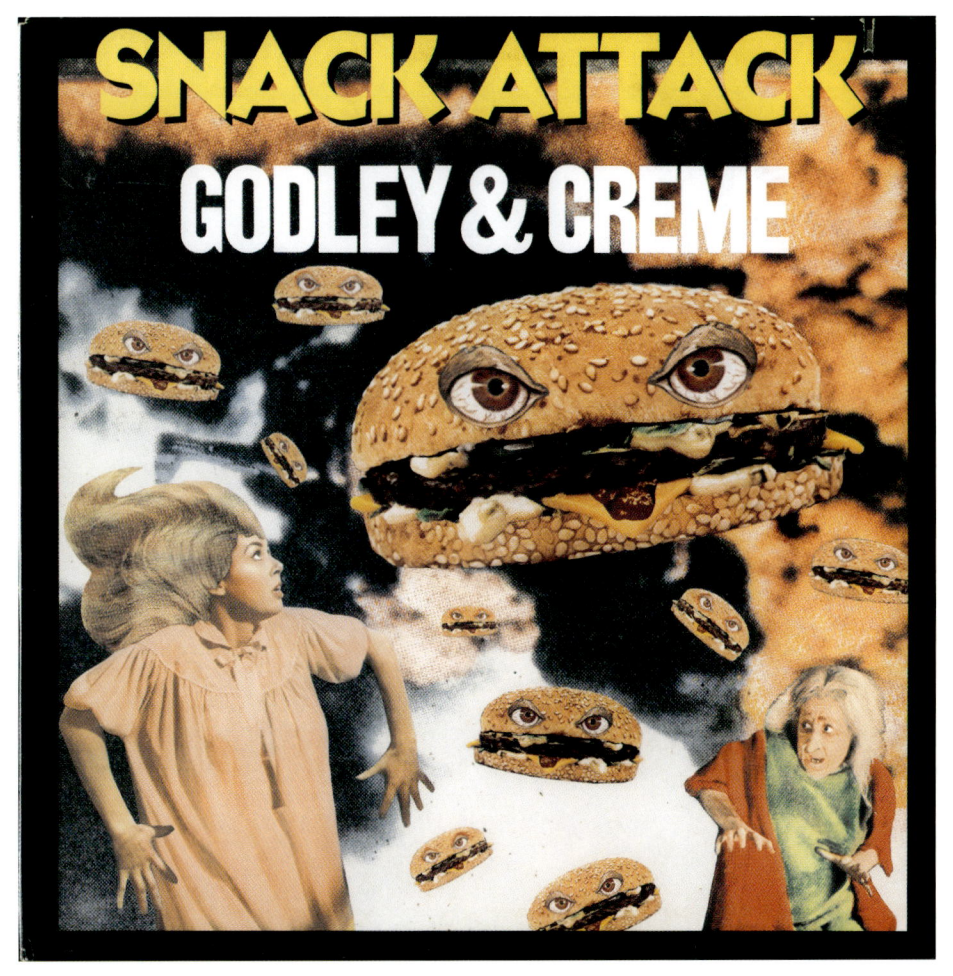

artist **GODLEY & CREME**
title **Snack Attack**

This horrific tableau of rampaging hamburgers is truly an American nightmare. I can only imagine the horrible night of heartburn and indigestion that prompted this design. Don't stare at this one too long, you'll wake up with a strange craving for french fries.

DON'T SMOKE DOPE, FRY YOUR HAIR!
Franklyn Ajaye

R RECOMMENDED FOR ADULT LISTENING

LD 1011

Little David

artist   **FRANKLYN AJAYE**
title   **Don't Smoke Dope, Fry Your Hair!**

This cover might actually be kind of cool if only Franklyn would put a shirt on! Of course that wouldn't help the title to make any more sense. The whole idea just sounds like a dangerous fire hazard to me!

artist **VARIOUS ARTISTS**
title **Las Aventuras De Enrique y Ana**
How is it that I have 250 cable TV channels, and I have still not seen this film? Someone in the programming department is not doing their job. Any movie that brings together an alien, an explorer, a lovable pre-teen heroine and a Miss Marple lookalike would surely be a worldwide hit.

18

South of the Border

In the 1950s' 'exotica' craze, record producers scoured the world for new, unfamiliar cultures to exploit. They needed to look no further than Mexico. In Mexico, men all wore huge sombreros, big, bright ponchos and strings of bullets. When not selling trinkets to tourists, they were busy drinking tequila and shooting guns.

At least, that's what you might think if all you had to go by was 1950s record albums. Luckily, modern American thrift stores hold a cornucopia of authentic 'south of the border' productions to set the record straight. Strangely, Mexican records are often better at promoting bad stereotypes than the American versions!

A TRAVELER'S GUIDE TO INSTANT SPANISH

artist **WILLIAM WHITBY**
title **A Traveler's Guide to Instant Spanish**
Here's the perfect record to prepare you for a trip south of the border. In order to purchase authentic native goods, you'll need to speak the lingo. 'How much does this cost?', 'Where is the bathroom?', 'How much Tequila can I smuggle home in my pants?'

188 • SOUTH OF THE BORDER

CONJUNTO AFRICA
CASATE JOSE

CASATE JOSE
LA CHAPARRITA
ESTAS APARTADA
COMO FUE
CUMBIA DE LA CADENITA
LINDO VERACRUZ
EL TODOPODEROSO
LOS BIKINIS
DISTANTE
AMOR NECIO

artist **CONJUNTO AFRICA**
title **Casate Jose**

Here we have a typical Mexican shotgun wedding. Actually, it's a shotgun, pistol and rolling pin wedding. This group at least knows how to have a good time when photographing an album cover!

El Duelo del Mayoral
EL INDIO DUARTE
Fuentes MF-3085

artist **EL INDIO DUARTE**
title **El Duelo del Mayoral**

There's nothing like an old-fashioned machete battle to get the blood pumping. It's unclear in the picture what these guys are fighting over. The guitar? The hat? Some unseen woman? I'm going to guess it's a woman. Few things get the machetes flying like a lady.

artist **LOS CHINACOS DE TONO MEDINA**
title **Que Siga la Fiesta**

If the machete battle wasn't gory enough for you, allow me to introduce the cockfight. It's fun for the whole family and good eating too. Although a popular tradition south of the border, cockfighting is sadly outlawed in the USA (except for the states of Louisiana and Oklahoma).

artist **"EL RIVEREÑO" PONCHO MARTINEZ**
title **Dispuesto a Morir**

Some album covers tell a story. Here we see Poncho. He has accidentally locked himself inside the gate of his apartment complex. Luckily, his wife has all the proper votive candles and, after a day of prayer, he is soon free to roam the city with his buddies.

192 • SOUTH OF THE BORDER

STEREO DS 399

POWER APPLE HONEY SERIES

LEMON TREE • GREEN EYES • LA BAMBA • THE HUNGRY BULL • MEXICAN JOE
MARGARITA • FIESTA • SOUTH SEA ISLAND MAGIC • SPANISH HARLEM • TAKE IT EASY

Si, Si, Señor BANDIDO

POCO LOCO GUITARS PLUS BRASS

artist **POCO LOCO GUITARS PLUS BRASS**
title **Si, Si, Señor Bandido**
This cover shows a typical Mexican breaking through the paper-thin US border and into your living room. Watch out! He's here to take your job! Maybe by playing this record, he'll let you live!

los xochimilcas
¡ hay naranjas !

SOMBRAS ★ HAY NARANJAS ★ PENICILINA ★ LA NEGRA ★ LA PAJARERA ★ MUSICA PARA MI REINA
EL AFILADOR ★ MI COMPADRE MANUEL ★ ACAPULCO ★ HEROICA VERACRUZ

artist **LOS XOCHIMILCAS**
title **¡Hay Naranjas!**
These guys really enjoy their oranges. A little too much, if you ask me. I'm not able to say why this scene is on their album cover, nor why they are all wearing cute outfits. I'm having a hard enough time pronouncing the band's name!

194 • SOUTH OF THE BORDER

VL 3600

PERCY FAITH
and his orchestra

LONG PLAY 33⅓
VOCALION
A PRODUCT OF DECCA RECORDS

North and South of the Border

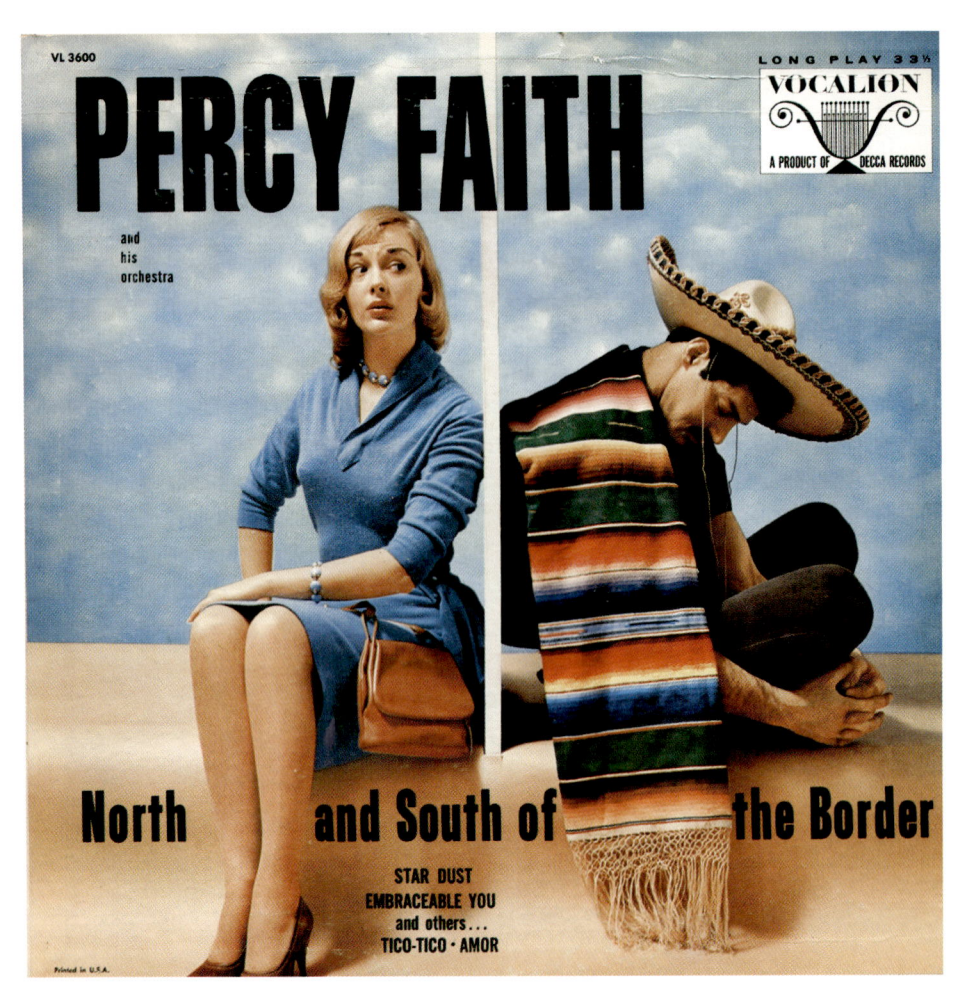

STAR DUST
EMBRACEABLE YOU
and others...
TICO-TICO • AMOR

Printed in U.S.A.

artist **PERCY FAITH**
title **North and South of the Border**

On one side of the border – the sexy, naïve young beauty, alert for any unwarranted incursions. On the other side, a snoozing native, too full of tequila to notice the blonde bombshell. He wants a job. She wants cheap prescription drugs. It's a match made in Laredo.

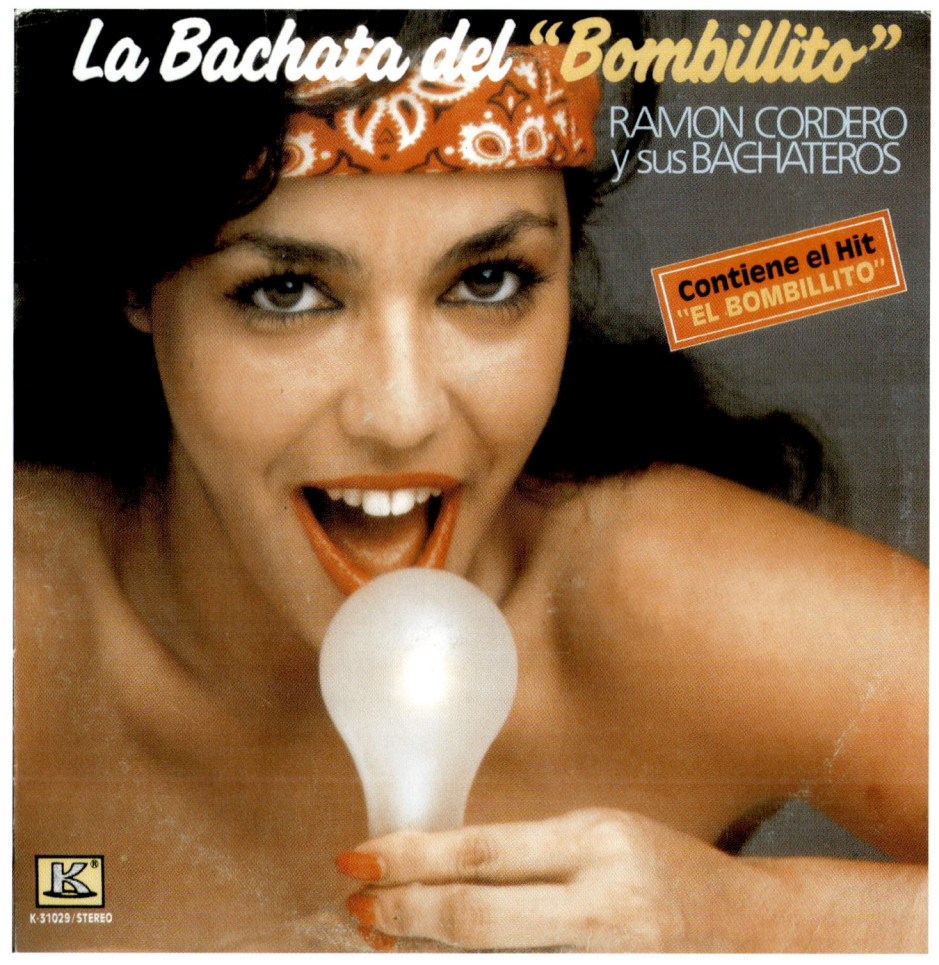

artist **RAMON CORDERO Y SUS BACHATEROS**
title **La Bachata del "Bombillito"**

Records from Mexico are not known for their subtlety. This is another in a series of records showing obviously thrilled models about to deep throat various objects. By this volume, they had used up the bananas and sausages and were down to using light bulbs!

19

Stretching Credibility

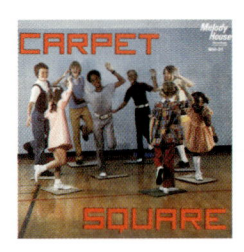

The endless variety of health and exercise records can basically be split into two eras: Before Jane Fonda and After Jane Fonda.

BJF records were dominated by buff, weightlifting men and flexible, ladylike women. In 1981, however, *Jane Fonda's Workout Record* sold millions, changing the world of exercise albums forever. Jane introduced Middle America to the flashy world of spandex tights and knit leg-warmers. Soon there was an exercise record for everyone, including pregnant women, Christians and small children.

Within a few short years, however, the aerobics craze was spent. Leotards were tucked away in the back of drawers and the legs of America became forever cold.

artist **RON HARRIS**
title **:20 Minute Workout**
Sometimes the exercise record ends up being more sexy that stretchy. At least I assume that's what this woman is trying to be with her poor-man's *Flashdance* routine. I'll bet the TV show was just as attention grabbing as this!

198 • STRETCHING CREDIBILITY

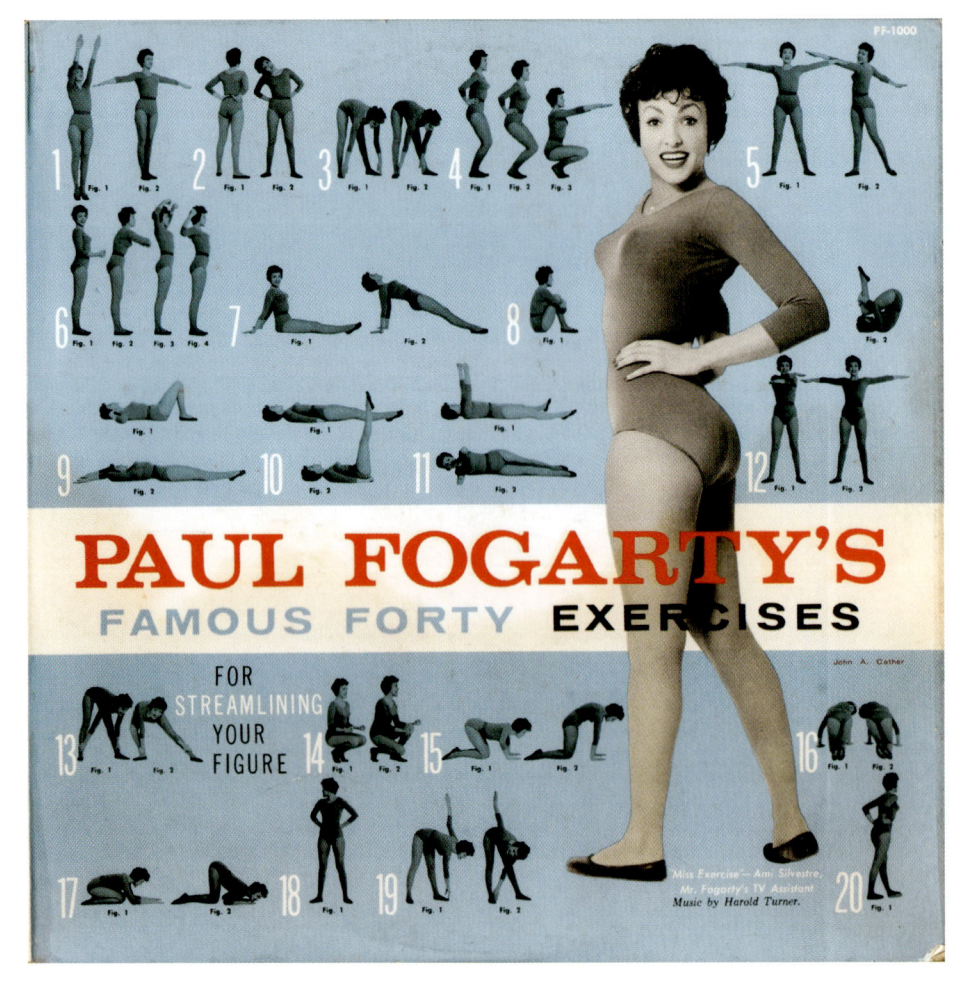

artist **PAUL FOGARTY**
title **Famous Forty Excercises**
In the 'olden days' of exercise records, the leotards were wool, the buns were steeled and the breasts were gravity-defying. Mr Fogarty probably thought he managed to sell so many records because of the effectiveness of his exercise. The cover designers knew different.

STRETCHING CREDIBILITY • 199

artist **DEBBIE DRAKE**
title **How to Keep Your Husband Happy**
Mid-century exercise records pulled no punches. You were doing this for one reason and one reason only – to please your man. As a male, it must have been nice to have a woman who cared nothing for her own health and happiness, but just yours. That's love, baby!

AEROBICS Country Style

Looking Good

LG 1009
Stereo

A basic program of Aerobic Dance and Exercise.

Featuring America's Most Popular Country Western Songs:

- Great Balls Of Fire
- Love in The First Degree
- 9 To 5 • Red Neckin'
- Take This Job And Shove It
- Fadin' In And Fadin' Out

artist **VARIOUS ARTISTS**
title **Aerobics Country Style**

Deftly combining the average American's love of useless exercise and crappy country music, Aerobics Country Style must have been a best-seller. It's like line-dancing in leotards, or boot-scooting for a better body. It's a win-win situation!

Gimnasia en su Hogar
por el profesor VELLANOWETH
VOLUMEN 2

HARMONY COLUMBIA lp
MONAURAL HL 8363

artist **PROFESOR VELLANOWETH**
title **Gimnasia en su Hogar Volumen 2**

It's no stretch to say that the exercise craze is a worldwide phenomenon. Meet Profesor Vellanoweth, the Mexican Richard Simmons. His TV exercise programme had señioritas swinging and stretching like Olympians.

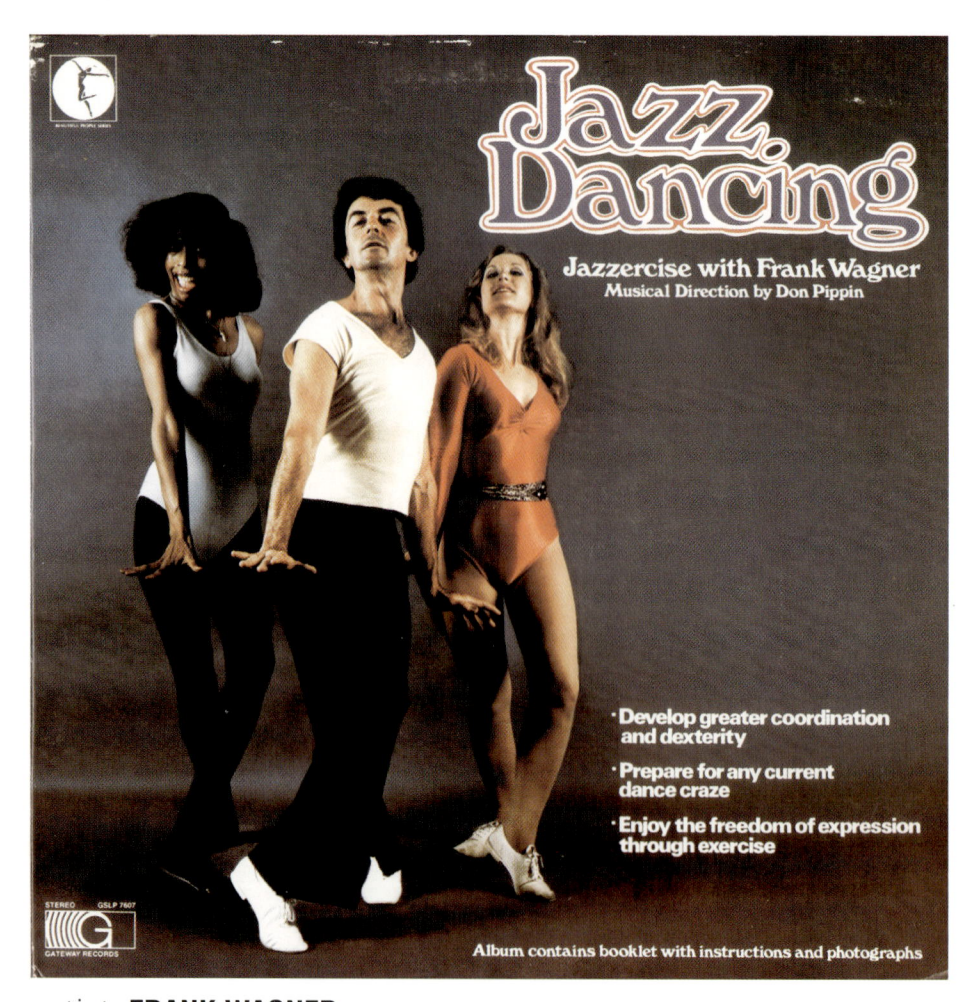

artist **FRANK WAGNER**
title **Jazz Dancing**

Learning to dance via an LP record is yet another strange concept from vinyl history. How on earth would you know if you were doing it right? Really, I think you need your own private, sweaty man in a leotard to learn properly. I suppose the advent of the video recorder helped a little.

artist **SHARRON L. LUCKEY**
title   **Carpet Square**

In my primary school PE class, we always had some gimmicky exercise. From parachutes to giant balls, no idea was too daft. I never had the chance to try the Carpet Square, but these kids seem to like it! The buildup of static electricity alone must have been frightening.

artist **IRLENE MANDRELL**
title **Texercise**

Few American states are egotistical enough to need their own exercise record. Not Texas. Everything is bigger here, including the waistlines. Luckily, Irlene is here with the 'Saddle Bag Stomp', 'The Pecos Pull' and 'Thighs of Texas' to get things back on track.

FIFTEEN FOR FITNESS

FIFTEEN MINUTES OF EXERCISE SET TO MUSIC
WITH INSTRUCTIONS AND CALLS By BOYD PEXTON – PRINCIPAL, FRANKLIN SCHOOL – SALT LAKE CITY, UTAH

THREE WARM-UP EXERCISES / SIX FUNDAMENTAL EXERCISES / SEVEN ADDITIONAL EXERCISES
Windsor Records WLP 3-06
Using exercises suggested by THE PRESIDENT'S COUNCIL ON PHYSICAL FITNESS

artist **BOYD PEXTON**
title **Fifteen For Fitness**

Ah, the American classroom of the 1950s. Notice the special atomic-bomb-proof desks filled with emergency food supplies. This is a Cold War era exercise record: after learning the 'duck and cover', these students are now learning the 'hands up and surrender'.

20

Teen Dance Party

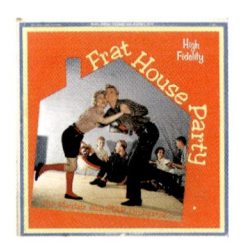

The full-length LP record was a dream come true for dance-partying teens. Now, a stack of records and a portable turntable meant hours of music! It was sort of like having an MP3 player, except 100 times heavier, with a lot less songs and bad sound.

In the early years, many of these 'teen' records were actually sub-standard cover versions of current hit songs. You've seen the term 'Original hits by the original artists' on compilation records? That's because of records like *12 Top Hits* that are neither of these things, the tunes being performed by unnamed studio musicians. Apparently the producers didn't think most teens would notice or care. Apparently most didn't!

STEREOPHONIC

✱ THE WORLD'S FINEST QUALITY STEREOPHONIC RECORD

Omega RECORDS

SWINGIN' NIGHT PEOPLE

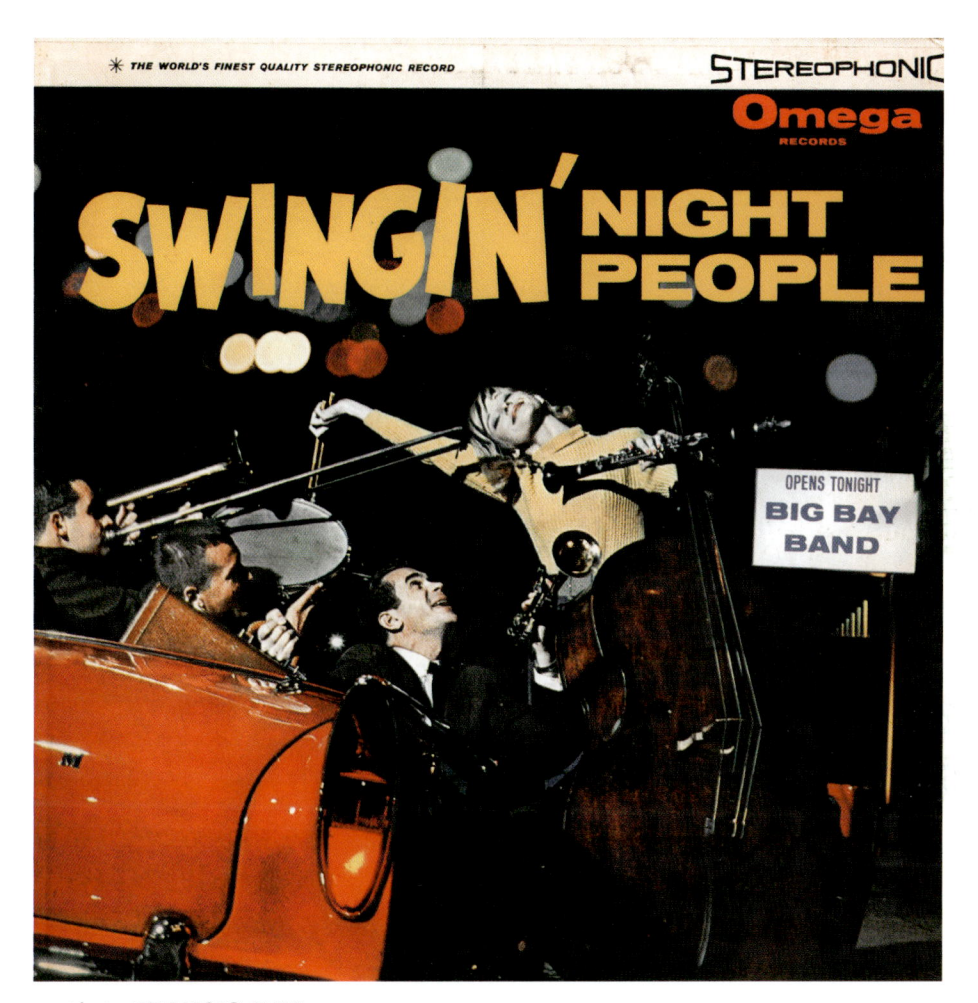

OPENS TONIGHT
BIG BAY BAND

artist   **FRANCIS BAY**
title   **Swingin' Night People**

      Wow, look at those crazy cats in the big city. They're out late on a school night, tearing up the town and stopping traffic. I would guess they're heading off to some hip party on the other side of town, full of artists and beatniks. Or maybe they just robbed a music store.

artist **THE BLAZERS**
title **College Drinking Songs**

The more things change, the more they stay the same. It's uncanny how students these days look exactly like this! This photo could be taken straight from a university website. The only difference is that they don't drink beer any more – it's just not considered 'cool' in the new century.

FULL FREQUENCY STEREO FULL FREQUENCY

TEEN AGE Dance Party

K131 GRAND PRIX SERIES

ONE O'CLOCK JUMP
DRAG RACE
C-JAM BLUES
PONY TAIL
TAKE THE "A" TRAIN
BOBBY SOX
STOMPIN' AT THE SAVOY
WIGGLE WALK
ROCKS AND ROLLS
TEEN DEEN

artist **BOBBY KRANE**
title **Teen Age Dance Party**
This girl looks so excited to finally be having her very own party! At the moment, she seems to only have two friends, and they're not paying much attention to her. She doesn't care! It's her party and she'll snap if she wants to.

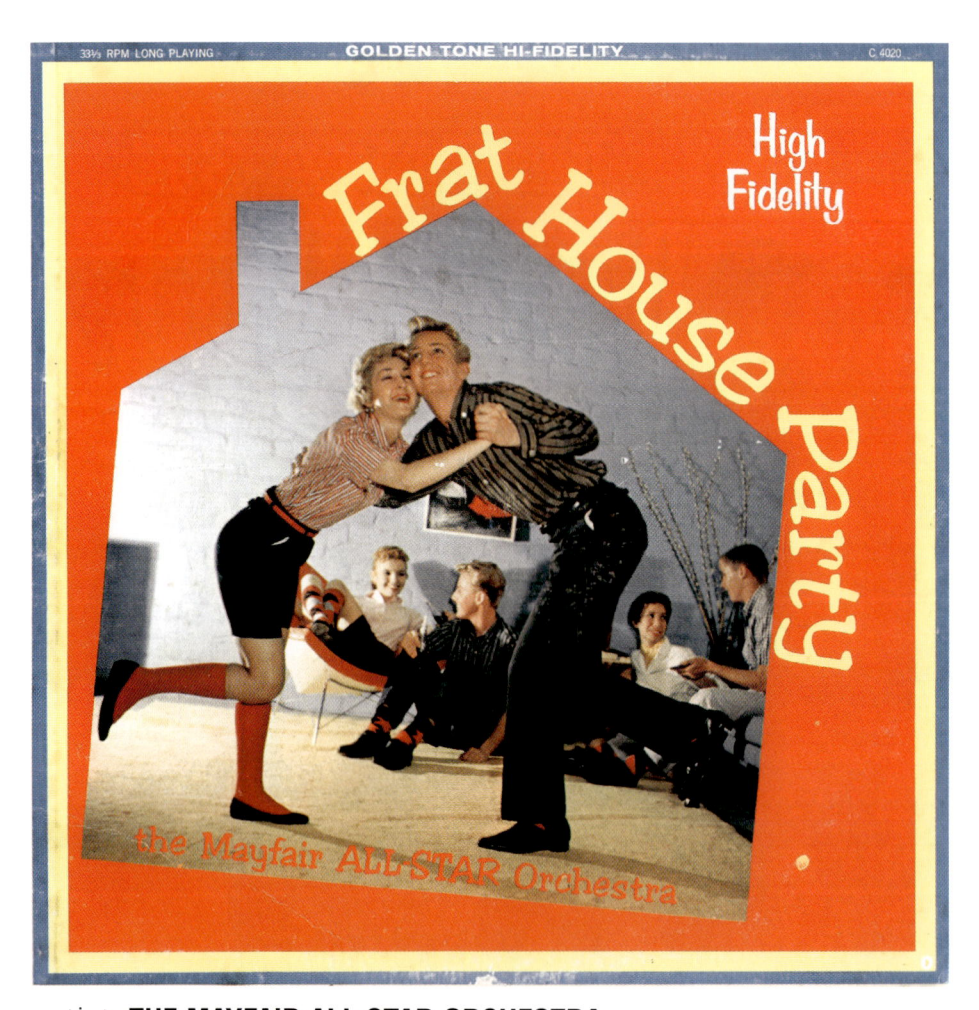

artist **THE MAYFAIR ALL STAR ORCHESTRA**
title **Frat House Party**

Outside of the major studios in the 1950s and 1960s were a variety of 'budget' labels. The musical selections were generally recorded by nameless studio musicians and sold in grocery and discount stores. A great album cover was needed and these guys spared no expense!

artist **VARIOUS ARTISTS**
title **12 Top Hits**

Here's a different record, on a different label. With the same carpet. The same brick wall. The same mod chairs. And the same goofy kids! What the heck, it's from the same photo shoot! In fact, you'll notice this 'white brick wall' set on the covers of many cheap-o records.

Hullabaloo Au-Go-Go!!!

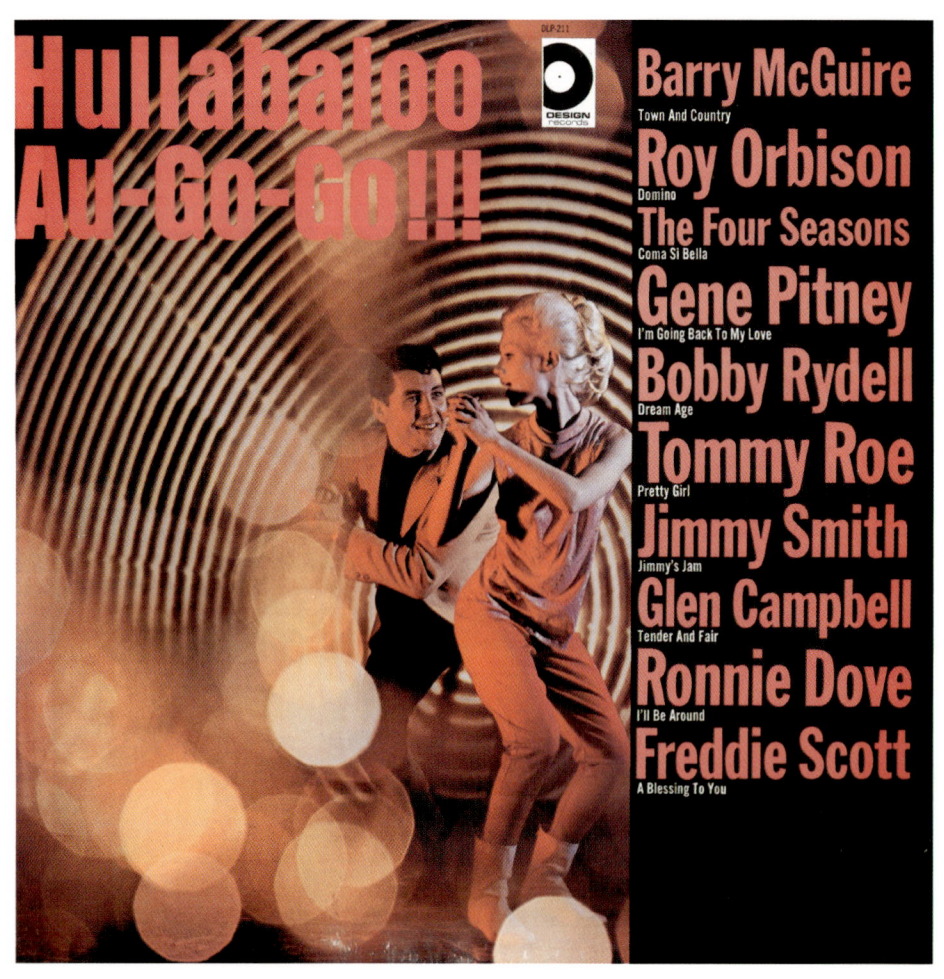

Barry McGuire — Town And Country
Roy Orbison — Domino
The Four Seasons — Coma Si Bella
Gene Pitney — I'm Going Back To My Love
Bobby Rydell — Dream Age
Tommy Roe — Pretty Girl
Jimmy Smith — Jimmy's Jam
Glen Campbell — Tender And Fair
Ronnie Dove — I'll Be Around
Freddie Scott — A Blessing To You

artist **VARIOUS ARTISTS**
title **Hullabaloo Au-Go-Go!!!**

In an effort to be 'hip', the latest styles and jargon were cobbled together by clueless old men into strange products, often resulting in a cover that has little to do with what's inside. How else could you sell this odd collection of random songs?

artist **VARIOUS ARTISTS**
title **12 Hit Parade Tunes**

We like to think of the 1950s as a sweet and innocent decade. But just look at the rampant debauchery evident on this album cover. The minds of the children are being corrupted by the gyrating hips and bosoms, while happy-hands at the table snuggles up to a much older woman. Scandalous!

21

Going Wild

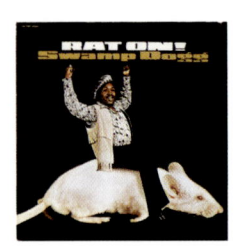

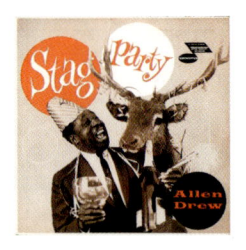

Animals have been an album cover staple for years. With a few exceptions, the animals do not actually perform on the record.

Lions are usually shown threatening young ladies. In the case of Tammy Faye's *Run Toward the Roar*, however, the lion simply looks a little bemused by her make-up. Gorillas have also been used on covers, principally for comic effect. It should be pointed out, however, that most of these are actually men in gorilla suits. Horses are used in a variety of poses. The rear end is the focal point of 'clown prince' Eli Basse's record. Redd Foxx gives us a similar view, but not being a butt expert, I am unable to confirm whether on not it is actually a horse…

Unfortunately, I cannot guarantee that no animals were harmed in the making of these album covers. Don't blame me – I just collect the things!

artist **THE DIXIE DOUBLE-CATS**
title **Is it True What They Say About Dixie?**

Is it true? In Dixie, do cats smoke cigarettes and wear ice bags on their heads? This looks like one of those internet photo sites where people have pictures of their pets passed out surrounded by beer bottles. Did this cat inhale?

artist **MIKE ADKINS**
title **Thank You For the Dove**

Does this man wander the forest, snatching birds from their nests? Or perhaps he is a 'fowl-whisperer', diagnosing the ills of avian pets. But if he invites you to dinner, you may discover what he really does with the birds!

BASSE-ACKWARDS

STARRING THE CLOWN PRINCE

ELI BASSE

AMERICA'S MOST FAMOUS GAG WRITER COMES FROM BEHIND THE SCENES WITH HILARIOUSLY FUNNY STORIES AND SNAPPY SONGS WRITTEN FOR THE GREAT COMEDY STARS

Stereo ODDITIES CB-1

NEW COMPATIBLE STEREO • PLAYS ON ANY PHONOGRAPH
PLAYS STEREO ON STEREO EQUIPMENT OR HI-FI (MONAURAL) ON HI-FI EQUIPMENT

artist **ELI BASSE**
title **Basse-Ackwards**

Here's another guy who uses poor, unsuspecting animals as the butt of his jokes. He appears to be trying out some sort of 'ass-bridle', which does not seem to have caught on generally. I believe that the horse was too embarrassed to show his face for the photographer.

artist **ALLEN DREW**
title **Stag Party**

Boy, this party looks like a blast! The ladies are gone, the dirty movies are on the projector and the strippers will be here at midnight! Have all the champagne you like, but please, please stay away from the stuffed deer. It's giving me the creeps.

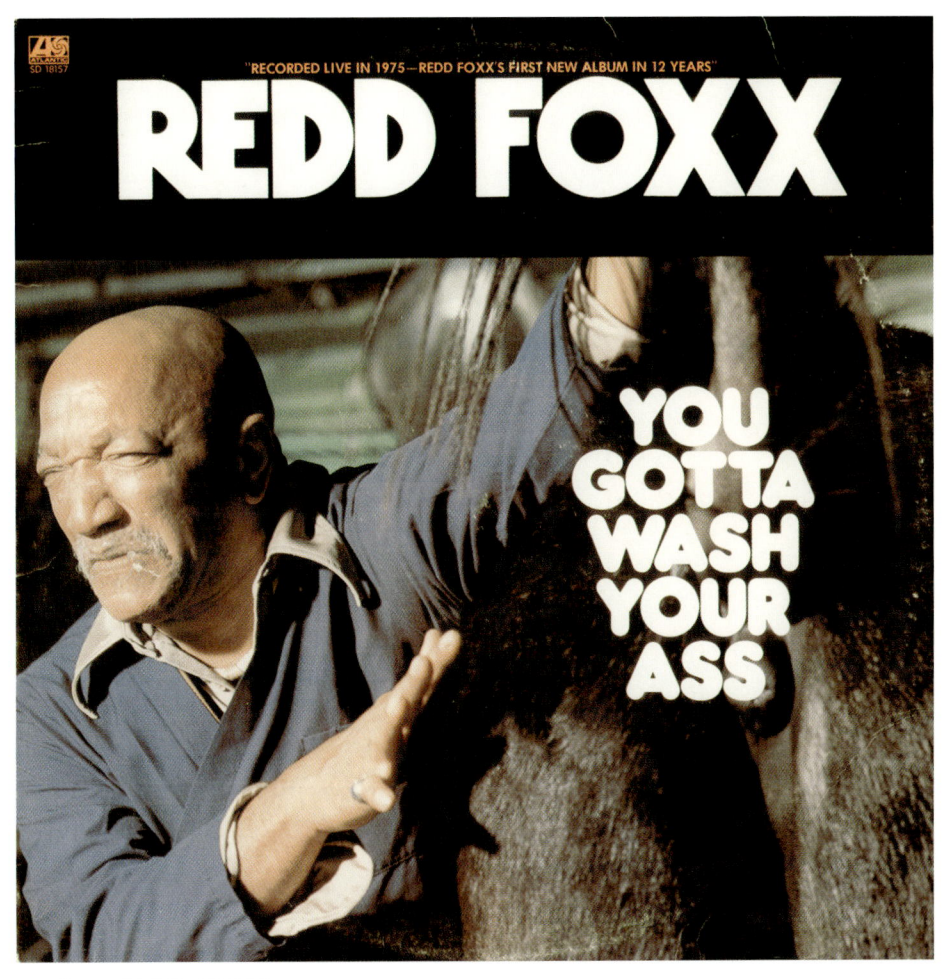

artist **REDD FOXX**
title **You Gotta Wash Your Ass**

Redd Foxx certainly knew how to approach the fine line between good and bad taste, and then take a running leap over it. The tracks on this record continue the fun with such gems as 'Both of Us Got Knives', 'You're Kind of Dumb and Ugly' and 'I Hate a Loud Broad'.

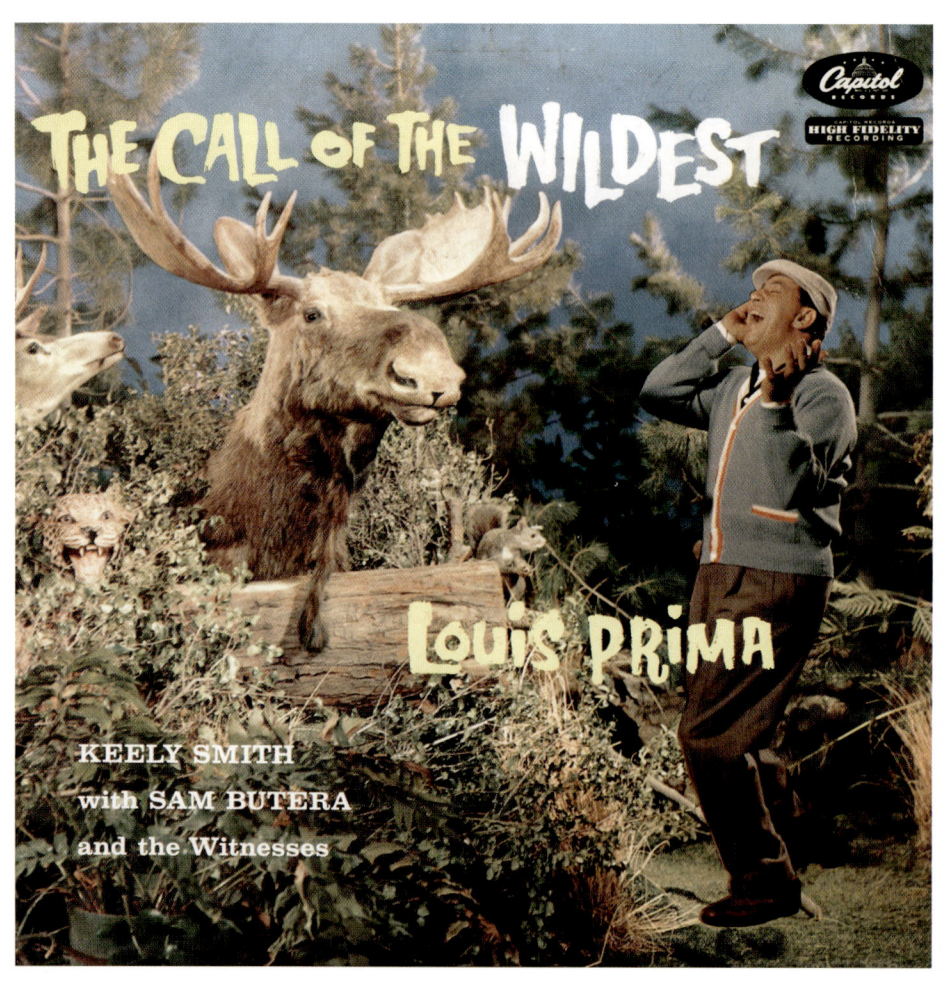

artist **LOUIS PRIMA**
title **The Call of the Wildest**

Big budget does not always mean big ideas. These designers obviously raided some executive's office for hunting trophies – let's hope they put them back before he returned from safari! So, if Louis Prima scats in the forest, does it make a sound?

artist **SWAMP DOGG**
title **Rat On!**

For some reason, rats seem to hold a certain fascination for many musicians. Here, Mr Dogg attempts to proclaim his superiority over the kingdom of the rat. I'm hoping that this is trick photography, but you never know!

artist **TAMMY FAYE**
title **Run Toward the Roar**

Tammy Faye (Bakker) is a Christian character of epic proportions. Her good-natured lunacy seems to know no bounds. I suppose when you own your own record label and television network, you can pretty much do whatever you want. And Tammy Faye certainly did!

FULL DIMENSIONAL STEREO

THEY SAID IT COULDN'T BE DONE!

BUT THEY DIDN'T RECKON WITH THE MIGHTY ACCORDION BAND

artist   **THE MIGHTY ACCORDION BAND**
title   **They Said it Couldn't Be Done!**

They said it couldn't be done… They said it shouldn't be done… They said it's the dumbest idea we've ever heard and some day this ridiculous, nonsensical cover will end up in a book about bad album covers… They were right.

22

Around the World

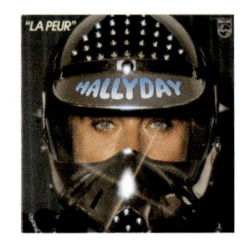

Records from other countries are rarely seen outside their native land. What might have been a No.1 hit in Estonia could be quite unknown outside the country's borders! Such records can usually be found only when a music lover moves to another country. I am always impressed that someone would choose to lug crates of records halfway around the world, yet I find it odd sometimes at the records they chose to bring. Did you really need that record of Chinese covers of classic country and western tunes?

artist **VARIOUS ARTISTS**
title **Moscow Nights**

Attention Party youth: Ve are now taking ze album cover photograph. You are to look happy and joyous at all times, Comrades. Failure to comply vill result in much unpleasantness. Ve have KGB agents stationed among ze revellers and vill know if you are not having the regulatory amount of fun.

artist **DOLLY ROLL**
title **Játék Az Élet...**

Records from 'foreign' nations are always a treat. You're never quite sure who these people are or what they're thinking. Is Dolly Roll, from Hungary, well-known there? Who's pulling their strings? Who's holding the scissors? Does everyone in Hungary wear red vinyl?

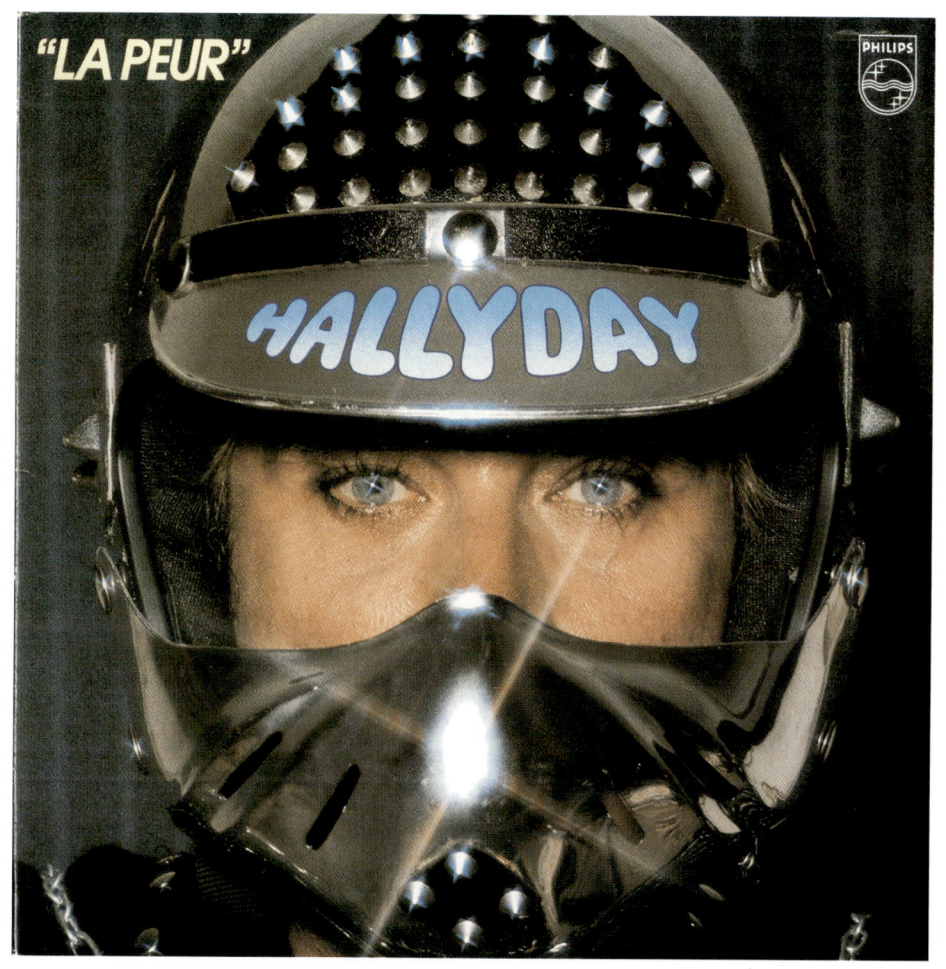

artist **JOHNNY HALLYDAY**
title **La Peur**

This record dates from the all-too-short 'Mad Max' era of rock 'n' roll – a style which didn't go too far beyond this record. Johnny is a French rock star, which does nothing to explain why he chose to imitate an Australian movie for this album cover.

artist **JIMMY JENSON**
title **Understand Your'e Swede**

Jimmy Jenson, back from a day chopping down very small trees and gathering a tiny bag of food, surveys his huge family. It's no surprise they have so many kids – his wife is certainly a hottie; she's even wearing a skirt out in the snow. But how on earth is he going to feed them all?

artist **PEPPI ECKMAIR**
title **Der Jodel-Peppi vom Schliersee**
A good yodelling record is a necessary souvenir from any trip to Bavaria. It's the gift that keeps on giving, every time you subject your friends and family to it. Luckily for the tourists, Peppi came down from the mountains long enough to play a few gigs and sign a few records.

artist **ORQUESTA DE LA LUZ**
title **Hot Salsa from Japan**

Bizarre musical combinations often lead to bizarre album covers, as this Venezuelan record of Japanese salsa music shows. The combination of Asian gongs, South American drums and naked Japanese men is sure to mean a good time.

artist **TERCET EGZOTYCZNY**
title **Tercet Egzotyczny**
A strange thing happened in Eastern Europe in the 1960s. The culture of Mexico suddenly became all the rage and Euro-Mex bands began popping up all over the place. This group seems to be doing their best despite a lack of Sombreros, traditional clothing and vowels.

Maxi 45 tours
Les 5 plus grosses bêtises des GARÇONS BOUCHERS

La Bière *(Nouvelle version)* - **Le Rap** *(Remix)*
Du Beaujolais *(Inédit)* - **Carnivore** - **Le Slow** *(Live)*

artist **LES GARÇONS BOUCHERS**
title **Les 5 plus grosses bêtises des Garçons Bouchers**
These butcher boys are real cut-ups as they try to look like the French Beastie Boys. One guy looks like he didn't get the memo, as he showed up with Flock-of-Seagulls hair and rainbow kiddie gloves. It's not hard to see why there are so few French rap stars!

artist **GERHARD POLT**
title **Leberkäs' Hawaii**

Here we have one of those album covers that is probably better left unexplained. Herr Polt may have a very good reason for perching his head atop a delicious plate of ham and pineapple. Then again, he may just be suffering from a case of Hawaii-envy.

23

A Very Vinyl Christmas

Since the dawn of recorded music, Christmas-themed releases have been an annual staple. Few artists have been able to resist the temptation to lend their talents to an interpretation of those well-known holiday classics. Artists think of Christmas as a time when they can make a quick record without the need to write anything. Record companies think of Christmas as a time when people are most likely to buy crap that they'll never actually listen to. Others know Christmas means lots of terrible album covers to collect!

artist **BORDER BRASS**
title **Tijuana Christmas**

As if torn from the pages of *National Geographic*, this cover is an authentic look inside the Mexican festival of 'Navidad'. From moustache to mittens, every detail of a Mexican Christmas has been painstakingly recreated.

236 • A VERY VINYL CHRISTMAS

artist **VARIOUS ARTISTS**
title **White Christmas**
Ah! Christmas in Korea. Could anything be more romantic? This cover shows an odd mix of crystal chandeliers, plastic swag, and disco fever. I'm not sure how they celebrate Christmas in Korea but it sure looks fun!

Rockin' Around The Christmas Tree / Good King Wenceslas / O Tannenbaum / White Christmas / Deck The Halls / The Twelve Days of Christmas / We Three Kings / Hark! The Herald Angels Sing / Auld Lang Syne

Yuletide Disco

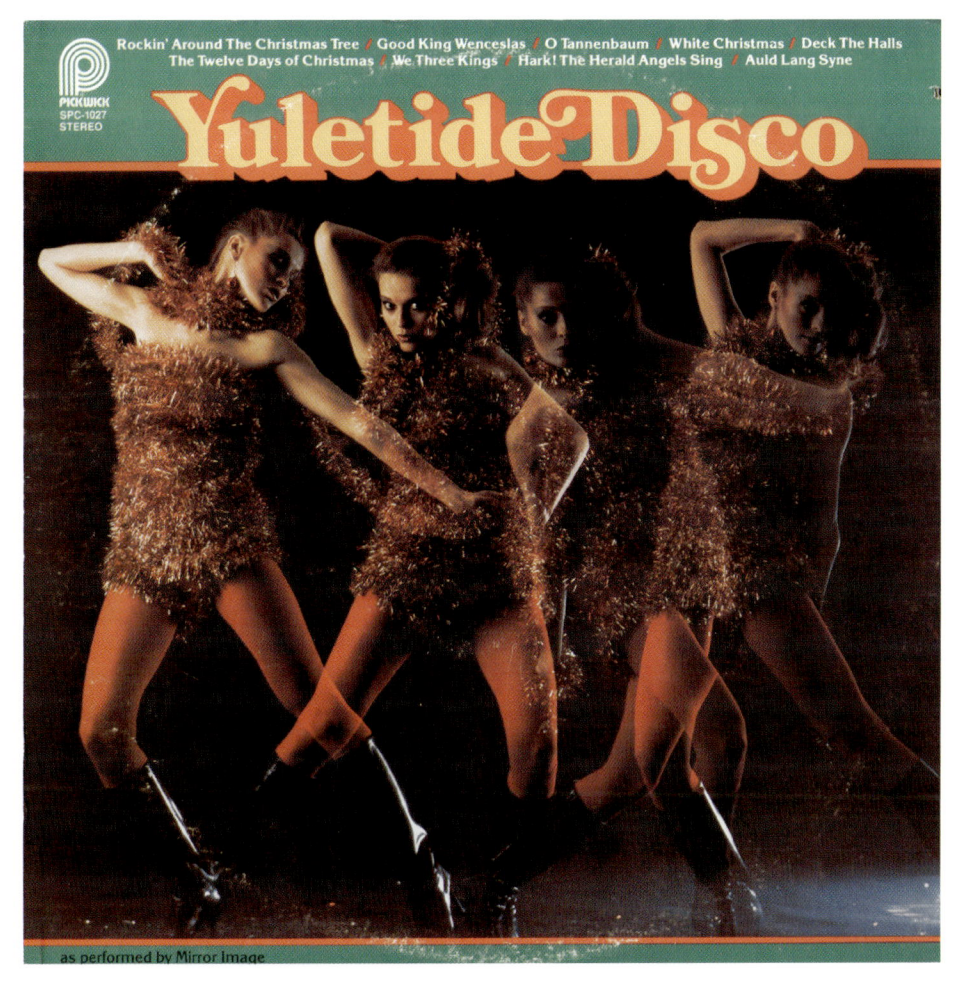

as performed by Mirror Image

artist **MIRROR IMAGE**
title **Yuletide Disco**

As if they weren't selling enough crappy disco records in 1979, *Yuletide Disco* was a must-have gift of the season. Chase the winter blues away with this platter of massacred Christmas songs and try out your holiday moves in the privacy of your own home.

artist **THE MOM AND DADS**
title **Merry Christmas**

Ah, that's more like it – a traditional family Christmas! The house is alive with the scamper of middle-aged men's feet and the smell of newly extruded polyester. Now that's what I call Christmas!

artist **SANTA'S HELPERS**
title **All I Want for Christmas is My Two Front Teeth**

What kids want for Christmas isn't always the best thing for them. One child wants a new bike but gets socks and underpants. Another kid who wants a video game gets educational software. This kid just wants his two front teeth, when what he really needs is a trip to the eye doctor.

artist **THE SURFERS**
title **Christmas from Hawaii**

In Hawaii, they have a legend. Every Christmas Eve, a boatload of four tanned hunks paddles around the world, stopping at the house of every boy and girl. If you've been naughty, you get a pineapple. If you've been nice, you get a wonderful gift, while your mother gets a back massage from one of them.

A SINGER Christmas for the family

WHITE CHRISTMAS
O COME ALL YE FAITHFUL
JOY TO THE WORLD
DECK THE HALLS
O HOLY NIGHT
SILENT NIGHT
THE FIRST NOEL
O LITTLE TOWN OF BETHLEHEM
AWAY IN A MANGER
HARK! THE HERALD ANGELS SING
GOD REST YE MERRY GENTLEMEN
WE WISH YOU A MERRY CHRISTMAS

THE MASTERTONE ORCHESTRA
featuring
THE DON JANSE CHORALE

*A Trademark of THE SINGER COMPANY.

artist **THE MASTERTONE ORCHESTRA FEAT. THE DON JANSE CHORALE**
title **A Singer Christmas for the Family**

The Singer Company knows what Mother wants for Christmas – another time-saving device that will inevitably only make more work for her. Little Suzie wants Mum to get cracking on some new doll outfits, while Junior looks very excited to have some new pajamas on the way.

STEREO STEREO

Christmas AT OUR HOUSE

RUDOLPH THE RED-NOSED REINDEER
THE FIRST NOEL
JOY TO THE WORLD
IT CAME UPON A MIDNIGHT CLEAR
SILENT NIGHT
O COME, ALL YE FAITHFUL
JINGLE BELLS
O LITTLE TOWN OF BETHLEHEM
GOD REST YE MERRY GENTLEMEN
WHITE CHRISTMAS
DECK THE HALL WITH BOUGHS OF HOLLY
AWAY IN A MANGER

MARTHA TILTON and other GREAT HOLLYWOOD vocal stars
GEORGE MATHER at the Console

TOPS Mayfair stereo

artist **VARIOUS ARTISTS**
title **Christmas At Our House**

Another example of an album cover photograph, shot on the warehouse loading dock, so popular with budget record labels. Apparently, at this house, Christmas involves no decorations whatsoever and the smallest possible train set you can buy. At least dad splurged on 10 square feet of carpeting.

Welcome To The World Of

Ann Guest Moore

artist **ANN GUEST MOORE**
title **Welcome to the World of Ann Guest Moore**
In the world of Ann Guest Moore, it's always Christmas time! On Christmas Eve, she's Santa's special elf, keeping up the spirits of the jolly man on his big night. The rest of the year, she spreads Santa's love through her nightclub act.

THE 'WHERE ARE THEY NOW?' FILE

It can be easy to forget that every record, no matter how unusual or obscure, has a person (or several) behind it. Some of these people are well-known, many are not, quite a few are still performing. Whatever the case, I have found an amazing number of interesting stories about the artists, simply by doing a little Internet research. I hope you enjoy reading the *'Where Are They Now?' File* as much as I did compiling it!

Tammy Faye Bakker (*Run Toward the Roar* – page 222):
Former wife and business partner of evangelist Jim Bakker, Tammy Faye has recently become something of a cult figure. An independent film, *The Eyes of Tammy Faye*, chronicled her life, and she appeared on the reality TV show, *The Surreal Life*, with Vanilla Ice and porn star Ron Jeremy. She is now re-married, writing books and fighting cancer.

Jim Bakker (*How To Accomplish the Impossible* – page 155):
Once the most powerful man in Christian evangelism, Bakker was convicted of fraud and tax evasion in 1993. After his release, he wrote a book entitled *I Was Wrong*, and now hosts another, albeit smaller, live TV show from Branson, Missouri.

LEFT: Sometimes an album cover might tell you something you really didn't want to know.

RIGHT: Captain Hook had big ideas but a small budget.

Rae Bourbon (*Let Me Tell You about My Operation* – page 50):

Rae/Ray Bourbon is one of the strangest characters in showbiz history. His recordings date back to the 1940s, and old 78rpm discs, when he was a popular cross-dressing entertainer, hanging out in Hollywood with the likes of Mae West and Bing Crosby. In 1956, his supposed sex change was announced in *Variety* magazine. After a decade of obscurity, he was convicted of hiring men to murder a kennel owner in Big Spring, Texas, in 1970. He died in prison in 1971.

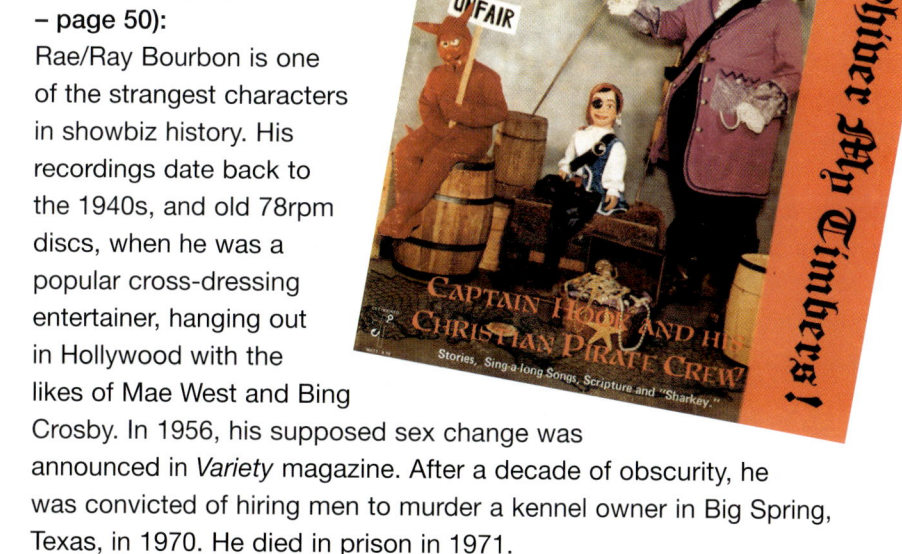

Elkie Brooks (*Rich Man's Woman* – page 165):

In the 1970s Elkie was in the band, Vinegar Joe, with Robert Palmer. She regularly tours in the UK and has been called 'one of the great British voices'.

Captain Hook and His Christian Pirate Crew (*Shiver My Timbers!* – page 22):

Information on the good Captain is scarce. I haven't even been able to find his real name. We do know that Hook, who had lost an arm and leg in a motorcycle accident, broadcast an extremely low-budget children's TV show from Indiana in the 1970s. His show featured his family and a crew of poorly-made puppets performing skits and promoting a strange view of Christianity.

Cepillin (*Un Dia Con Mamá* – page 19):
Ricardo Gonzalez, aka Cepillin, was a Mexican dentist who donned make-up and wig to amuse the children during exams; the name Cepillin means 'little toothbrush'. In the 1970s, he was the star of his own hugely popular television show. He now runs a circus that performs in Mexico.

Cynthia Clawson (*You're Welcome Here* – page 107):
Called 'The most awesome voice in gospel music' by *Billboard* magazine, the Grammy-winning Clawson is now pastor of a church in Austin, Texas.

Ken Demko (*Live at the Lamplighter Inn* – page 129):
Ken is now a church organist in Lakewood, Ohio.

Devastatin' Dave, The Turntable Slave (*Zip Zap Rap* – page 54):
Dave Cary lives in Los Angeles, and is working on his full-length album *Havin' a Dream*.

Dolly Roll (*Játék Az Élet...* – page 226):
Stand-outs in the surprisingly crowded genre of Hungarian rock 'n' roll, Dolly Roll have released over 25 albums since 1983. They regularly perform for crowds of 100,000 fans, and wrote the music for Hungary's 1996 Olympic team. One notable record is a 1992 duets album with American rockabilly queen Wanda Jackson, featuring such classics as 'Let's Have a Party', 'Rip It Up', and the ever-popular 'Jojj Vissza'. Now there is a record that I *must* find!

Dr. Jerry Falwell (*Where Are the Dead?* – page 163):
Falwell is a notorious TV evangelist, currently best known for his controversial theories and utterances. In 1999, he rocked the world of children's television with allegations of the homosexual agenda of Tinky Winky, the Teletubby. In September 2001, he accused 'abortionists, feminists, and gays' of contributing to the World Trade Center attack. He regularly appears on US TV as an 'expert': at what, remains unclear.

Arthur Fiedler (*Saturday Night Fiedler* – page 40):
This legendary conductor led the Boston Pops orchestra from 1930 until his death in 1979.

Foggy River Boys (*I Believe In Music* – page 69):
The Boys held court at the Foggy River Boys Theater in Branson, Missouri for 23 years. They played their final performance in July 2002.

Miss Frances (*Ding Dong School* – page 16):
The Ding Dong School television show aired on US network television from 1952 to 1965. Miss Frances went on to be the NBC network's Supervisor of Children's Programs. After her death in 2001, an auction of *Ding Dong School* memorabilia was held to the delight of Ding Dong collectors everywhere.

Johnny Hallyday
(*La Peur* – page 227):
Hallyday is the biggest – and pretty much *only* – French rock star. He shot to fame in the early days of rock 'n' roll as 'The French Elvis', playing French covers of American hits. As an enduring public figure, Hallyday has sold over 100 million records, starred in dozens of films, and is a fixture on French TV. And yet he remains virtually unknown outside of France. In 2005, he had his 33rd no.1 single.

RIGHT: Some album covers are nothing more than pretty pictures. Others, aren't.

Arthur Holst (*The Challenge of A Pro* – page 87):
After 15 years and two Super Bowls as an official in the National Football League, Mr Holst is now a motivational speaker.

Hello People (*Bricks* – page 145):
The Hello People are the undisputed originators of the sub-sub-genre of music known as 'Mime Rock'. Apparently the band performed standard hippy rock numbers, with mime routines between songs. Although they played to national TV audiences on the *Johnny Carson* and the *Smothers Brothers* shows, the Hello People never found stardom, and drifted off to wherever it is old mime rockers drift off to.

High Noon (*Bendin' Rules & Breakin' Hearts* – page 27):
These boys are alive and well and still rocking rural Minnesota. They are available to play at your wedding and other special occasions.

The HOT Czechs (*Goin' Bankin'* – page 140):
The Heart of Texas Czechs began as a 'garage polka' band playing at a family reunion in 1979. They played for five years, but released only one album. The band's leader, Ronnie Hurta, presently has a CD available called *The Lone HOT Czech Plays Again*, on which he plays classic Czech polkas on his computer.

LEFT: The Hello People developed their own musical genre, which was known as 'Mime Rock'.

RIGHT: Millie Jackson's record is undeniably one of the worst album covers ever!

Millie Jackson (*Back to the S_ _t!* – page 170):
Millie Jackson is a controversial R&B singer who has released over 20 albums since the early 1970s. Her explicit lyrics and 'risque' album covers have hindered mainstream acceptance of her music, although she has recently been recognized by rap artists as 'the mother of hip-hop'. Millie has released a new album, *Not For Church Folk* with the single 'Butta-Cize'. She owns a recording studio in Dallas.

Jeff (*Something Special* – page 157):
Jeff Steinberg was tragically born without arms and with deformed legs. In spite of his disabilities, he has gone on to become a busy gospel singer and public speaker. He also wrote a comedy routine about being drafted into the military.

Kreskin (*The Basic Principles of Kreskin's ESP* – page 93):
Also known as George Kresge, Kreskin is a popular 'mentalist' who has appeared on countless television and radio shows and even on *The Simpsons*. His New Year's Day predictions on CNN have become a traditional feature of the season.

LEFT: Do Beverly and Erick have secret knowledge of the JFK assassination?

Eddie Layton (*Organ Moods in Hi-Fi* – page 134): Layton became the organist for the New York Yankees in 1967, retiring in 2003 as a household name in the Big Apple. He died in December 2004.

Beverly Massegee (*Amen!* – page 21): Ms Massegee claims to be the mysterious 'babushka lady' – the be-scarved young woman who was photographed apparently filming JFK at the very moment at which he was assassinated, but was never positively identified. Massegee made her claim to JFK researcher Gary Shaw in 1970 and told him that the FBI had taken away her film. 'I wasn't smart enough to ask for a receipt,' she explained in 1994. By that time she had taken up the art of ventriloquism and married a Baptist minister.

Arthur Murray (*Cha Cha* – page 35):
Known as 'the man who taught America to dance', Arthur Murray developed his trademark 'footprints' diagrams, showing his students where to place their feet for various dance steps. He also began to franchise his name to other dance studios, and his company still exists today. His television show in the 1950s was very popular and spawned dozens of records, each demonstrating the latest dance steps. He died in 1991.

Orquesta de la Luz (*Hot Salsa from Japan* – page 230):
This group has been called the best salsa band ever to come out of Japan. (There *was* another one – I checked.) The following info is from the band's website, put through one of those automatic translation programs: 'It forms in Tokyo fall of 1984. 1990 year first album the (ocean subject from the monkey whose is hot). It becomes the heroic deed which from now on 11 weekly it continues keeps.' Now that we know all about the band, let's get to work on improving Internet translation technology...

Larry Rivera (*A Nite Cap With Larry* – page 77):
Larry has worked at the Coco Palms resort in Kaua'i since 1951, when he was hired to wait tables and sing. The resort was largely destroyed by Hurricane Iniki in 1992. Rivera performs Elvis-themed 'Blue Hawaii' weddings on the grounds to this day.

LuLu Roman (*Now Let Me Sing* – page 110):
Known (briefly) as America's Sweetheart, LuLu was a regular cast member on the *Hee-Haw* show in the 1970s. She also writes cookery books.

Anna Russell (*In Darkest Africa* – page 178):
Canadian songstress and comedienne, Russell is retired and living in Australia. She has a street named after her in Toronto, Canada.

The Stellar Unit (*The Stellar Unit* – page 81):
After a long hiatus, the Nerdy Three are back and can be seen playing shows in Houston, Texas.

Sunshade 'n Rain (*Naturally* – page 68):
If you were lucky enough to be at the 2005 Utah State Fair, you could have seen Sunshade 'n Rain perform Monday night, opposite the Cook's Racing Pigs show.

The Surfers (*Christmas from Hawaii* – page 240):

The Surfers biggest moment came in 1961, when they recorded with Elvis Presley on the soundtrack to the film *Blue Hawaii*. The band's founding member Alan Naluai died in 2001 of heart disease. However, in March, 2005, the remaining Surfers reformed to play a charity benefit for the American Heart Association.

Thor (*Keep The Dogs Away* – page 150):

Jon Mikl Thor was a champion bodybuilder as a youth, but turned to a career in glam metal in 1977. Of late, he has acted in several horror movies, co-authored a comic book (*Thor vs. Beastwomen from the Center of the Earth*) and still tours with his band. 'Blowing up hot water bottles, bending steel, and having cinder blocks broken over his chest are all in a night's work,' claims his bio.

Roger Troutman (*The Many Facets of Roger* – page 61):

Roger Troutman and his brothers founded the revolutionary funk band Zapp in 1980. Troutman was known for his use of the vocoder or 'talk box', a vocal synthesizer with a breath tube that provides a wah-wah sound, which he called 'the ghetto robot'. His bid for a hip hop comeback came to a tragic end on 25th April 1999 when he was found shot to death in his recording studio in Dayton, Ohio.

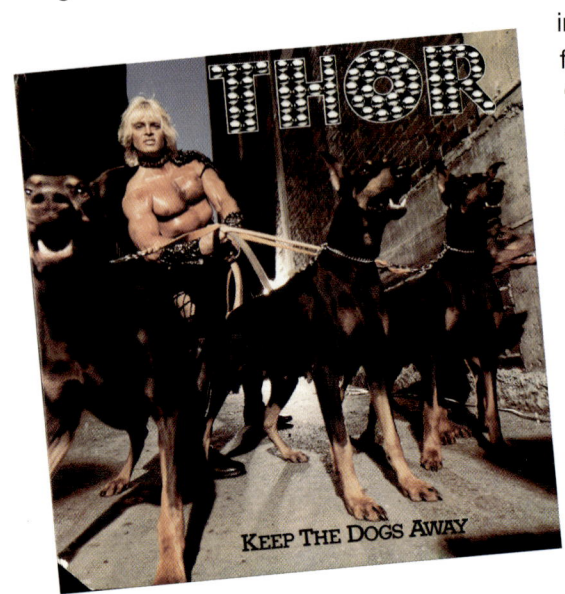

LEFT: Thor is a man who loves his music, his dogs and his fabulous pectorals.

RIGHT: Merrill Womach talks about his horrible plane crash on this record.

Dr. Jack van Impe (*Hell Without Hell – Is It The Grave?* – page 162):
Jack and wife Rexella are still preaching about the imminent end of the world, as they have for over 50 years, on their weekly news-style television show.

Johnny 'Guitar' Watson (*What The Hell Is This?* – page 57):
This legendary blues guitarist from Houston died on stage in 1996 during a comeback tour in Yokohama, Japan. He was playing 'Superman Lover'.

Justin Wilson (*Whoooooo Boy!!!* – page 33):
Justin Wilson, from Roseland, Louisiana, brought the unique French-American 'Cajun' culture of his childhood to the world. As a comedian, he released over two dozen records. In the 1980s, he became known to millions as 'The Cookin' Cajun' on his TV chef show. His catchphrases 'I gar-on-tee' and 'How y'all are' have become Cajun clichés. He died in 2001.

Merrill Womach (*Happy Again* – page 159):
Merrill was a gospel singer before being horribly burned in a tragic 1961 aeroplane crash. Then his career really took off. Presently, he runs a large company in Spokane, Washington, which provides music and video services to funerals.

FURTHER INFORMATION

Artists' Websites

Franklyn Ajaye:
franklynajaye.com

Jim Bakker:
jimbakkershow.com

Tammy Faye Bakker:
tammyfaye.com

Bowley & Wilson:
bowleyandwilson.com

Oscar Brand:
oscarbrand.com

Elkie Brooks:
elkie-brooks.com

Cynthia Clawson:
cynthiaclawson.com

Dolly Roll:
dollyroll.hu

Happy Louie:
happylouie.com

High Noon:
highnoon.to

Art Holst:
artholst.com

Millie Jackson:
weirdwreckuds.com

Jeff:
tinygiant.com

Kreskin:
amazingkreskin.com

Beverley Massegee:
massegee.org

Northams:
northams.org

Orleans:
orleansonline.com

Gerhard Polt:
polt.net

Jim Post:
jimpost.com

Mr. Rogers:
pbskids.org/rogers

LuLu Roman:
luluroman.20m.com

Swamp Dogg:
swampdogg.net

Thor:
thorcentral.com

Justin Wilson:
justinwilson.com

Other Websites

The Author's Site:
BizarreRecords.com

Kiddie Records Weekly:
kiddierecords.com

Christmas Records:
falalalala.com

Whistling Records:
whistlingrecords.com

The Knockoff Project:
knockoffproject.com

Belly Dance Records:
radiobastet.com

Yu-Mex Records:
friends.s5.net/mazzini/ovitki/

ACKNOWLEDGEMENTS

All the album covers featured are from the author's collection.

The publishers would like to thank all artists and recording companies who agreed to be included in the book. Every effort was made to contact the parties concerned with the copyright of these album covers.

Gerhard Polt, *Leberkäs' Hawaii* appears courtesy Jupiter-Records, Germany.
Jim Post, *I Love My Life* used by permission of Stephen Powers and Mountain Railroad Records.

*

Thanks to Alison, Matt, Morton and Alicia, Chris DiFonzo, Jim and Helen, my parents, and everyone else who has found records for me! Thanks to the artists for putting these records out, and thanks also to everyone at New Holland for the opportunity to write this book.

First published in 2006 by New Holland Publishers (UK) Ltd
London • Cape Town • Sydney • Auckland

www.newhollandpublishers.com

Garfield House, 86–88 Edgware Road, London W2 2EA, United Kingdom

80 McKenzie Street, Cape Town 8001, South Africa

14 Aquatic Drive, Frenchs Forest, NSW 2086, Australia

218 Lake Road, Northcote, Auckland, New Zealand

2 4 6 8 10 9 7 5 3

Copyright © 2006 in text: Nick DiFonzo
Copyright © 2006 in photographs: as credited on page 255
Copyright © 2006 New Holland Publishers (UK) Ltd

All rights reserved. No part of this publication may be reproduced, stored in any retrieval system or transmitted, in any form or by any means, electronic, mechanical, photocopying, recording or otherwise, without the prior written permission of the publishers and copyright holders.

ISBN-10: 1 84537 589 0
ISBN-13: 978 1 84537 589 8

Publishing Manager: Jo Hemmings
Editor: Gareth Jones
Assistant Editor: Kate Parker
Designer: Gülen Shevki-Taylor
Production: Joan Woodroffe

Reproduction by Modern Age Repro House Ltd, Hong Kong
Printed and bound by Craft Print International Pte Ltd, Singapore

Publisher's Note:
Every effort has been made to contact the parties concerned with the copyright of these album covers. Any further information pertaining to copyright will be included in future editions.